The National Trust Year Book 1977-78

Europa Publications Limited
18 Bedford Square, London, WC1B 3JN

© The National Trust
ISBN: 0 905118 16 2

Printed and bound in England by
Staples Printers Limited
at The George Press, Kettering, Northamptonshire

The National Trust Year Book 1977-78

Studies in Art History
and
Nature Conservation
relating to Properties in the care of
the National Trust

Published for the National Trust by Europa Publications
London

Cover: Detail from the *Adoration of the Magi*, by Ludovico Cardi
called 'Il Cigoli' (1559–1613), painted in 1605.
(National Trust, Stourhead, Wiltshire).

Contents

Foreword

The articles in this, the third *Year Book* to be published by the National Trust, once again cover a broad spectrum of different interests. Reflecting in part the immensely wide range of the Trust's own activities, it is hoped that this will be interpreted as a sign of its continuing strength. Despite the scholarship and first-hand research that has gone into this writing, these essays on aspects of the country house, its contents and its landscape setting, are intended to interest the many general readers rather than the few specialists among our 500,000 members. The subjects treated this year include paintings, sculpture and wood-carving, natural history, horticulture and landscape gardening, architecture and (in the case of Mr. Brinsley Ford's article on Wyndham Ketton-Cremer) personal reminiscences.

We are particularly grateful to Mr. Ford, not only for his fascinating character-study of one of the most generous of all the Trust's benefactors, but for portraying so vividly the tenor of life at Felbrigg in the 'Squire's' day. We also hope that this will be the first of a series of similar articles, in future Year Books, on the life led by owners of National Trust houses in the period before they passed out of private hands, still easily within living memory, but all too easily unrecorded and finally forgotten. Another article on an individual, Mrs. Lees Milne's study of Lawrence Johnston, must also be mentioned for the light it casts on the hitherto shadowy, retiring character of the creator of the famous gardens at Hidcote.

Miss Karin Walton's survey of housekeeping in the eighteenth and nineteenth centuries is of particular topical interest, now that the conservation of rare furniture and textiles has become such an important issue, and a return is being made in many National Trust houses to the old system of 'case covers' for chairs, and leathers for elaborate table tops. The comprehensive survey of the park and gardens at Dyrham by Anthony Mitchell is also of particular relevance, since the 274 acre park was acquired by the Trust and opened to the public only last year. The contemporary description of the gardens by Stephen Switzer, which is published as an appendix, illustrated by the relevant details from Kip's famous view of Dyrham, establishes William Blathwayt's as perhaps the best documented Baroque garden layout in this country.

Since Dr. Smart's article on Wicken Fen was written, there has been welcome news that the attempts to reintroduce the Swallowtail butterfly, which he describes, appear to have been successful. Frequent sightings of butterflies were reported in early July (delayed because of the late summer) and Dr. J. P. Dempster's team from the Institute of Terrestrial Ecology also found some eggs in their transects. The fact that this rare butterfly did survive the severe drought of last summer raises considerable hope that it will be able to maintain itself on the fen in future years.

The Trust is grateful to these and all the other contributors to this volume—particularly those who have generously offered to do so without remuneration. Thanks must also go to our publishers, both for their help at every stage in the preparation of this book, and also, with the costs of paper and printing rising so rapidly, for continuing to give us their support.

Gervase Jackson-Stops

Cigoli's Adoration of the Magi at Stourhead

TIMOTHY CLIFFORD

Above the chimneypiece in the picture gallery at Stourhead, Wiltshire, hangs Cigoli's *Adoration of the Magi* (Fig. 1).[1] Despite the painting's prominent size and easy accessibility in a much visited house, its whereabouts have often been overlooked, and it has never been the subject of a detailed published study.[2] The picture is of particular interest for we know the Florentine church and the family chapel for which it was commissioned, the probable circumstances of that commission, and the special significance of the subject matter. Through the many surviving preparatory drawings we can follow the artist's creative processes and, from early descriptions, build up an idea of the altarpiece's original setting. During the artist's lifetime the picture was considered a masterpiece and influenced other Florentine artists. In the late eighteenth century it was sold from the church and bought by Sir Richard Colt Hoare of Stourhead, then on the Grand Tour. Back at Stourhead the picture dictated the overall height and (with other pictures in the collection) the proportions and exterior elevation of the new picture gallery.

Ludovico Cardi (1559–1613), called 'Il Cigoli' (Fig. 2) from his birthplace near Florence, is usually considered one of the principal reformers of the ideals of the High Renaissance and as a precursor of the Baroque.[3] In reacting against Mannerism he fulfils a similar role in Florence to the Carracci in Bologna, Cerano in Milan and the Lombard Caravaggio in Rome. His art is built on the solid foundation in design of his masters Alessandro Allori and Santi di Tito; to this is added the sprightly elegance and imagination of his other master Bernardo Buontalenti. Cigoli shows in his works an admiration for Leonardo's handling of light, Correggio's figure types, and the realism and feminine spirituality of Barocci. Cigoli's palette is however essentially Florentine with a relatively harsh use of local colour. His paintings are not so much charged with Counter-Reformation fervour as they are serious, sombre and, on appropriate occasions, gently pietistic.

Cigoli subscribed to the ideal of the universal man and combined an expertise in mathematics, anatomy, music and architecture. He wrote poetry, a treatise on perspective, played the lute and competed for the façade design of St. Peter's, Rome. A close friend of Galileo, he was apparently the first artist to paint a picture of the moon with its craters.[4] As one of the court painters to the Grand Duke, Cigoli designed tapestries, prepared cartoons for the 'pietra dura' industry, invented costumes for masques and devised temporary decorations for triumphs and obsequies. He was elected a member of the Accademia della Crusca and dubbed a Knight of Malta.

Sir Richard Colt Hoare of Stourhead (1758–1838) (Fig. 3) recorded in the description of his house in *The Modern History of Wiltshire* that he had bought in Florence Cigoli's *Adoration of the Magi* in 1790 and that it had come from the Albizzi Chapel in the Church of S. Pier Maggiore.[5] This Gothic church, which belonged to an order of Benedictine nuns, was situated at the eastern end of the Borgo degli Albizzi, very close to Palazzo Albizzi, south-east of the Duomo.[6] It was one of the earliest and most splendid churches in Florence and boasted many masterpieces of Tuscan painting and sculpture, some of which later found their way to England.[7] The church's fabric by the eighteenth century was clearly in a poor state and on 9 July 1784 after lunch, half the roof collapsed.[8] The nuns moved to other quarters in the city, and although for several years the guidebooks reported that the church was to be restored, it must soon have been apparent that this was a forlorn hope. In fact, the roof's collapse could not have been more conveniently timed, as Florence teemed with English collectors whose delight in relieving the local inhabitants of their treasures was matched only by the locals' delight in relieving them of their money. All that remains of

1. 'The Adoration of the Magi' by Ludovico Cardi called 'Il Cigoli' (1559–1613), 1605. Canvas 346 × 234 cm. (National Trust, Stourhead, Wiltshire).

the building today is the tripartite triumphal arch motif of the early seventeenth century façade in 'pietra serena' with Corinthian pilasters supporting three arches and a boldly moulded entablature (Figs 4 and 5). Through the central arch and down what was the nave runs the Via S. Piero Maggiore, while houses and shops cluster behind the blind arches where the aisles and side chapels once stood. In front of the façade is the Piazza S. Piero, usually filled with the picturesque clutter of a vegetable market.

The church's original exterior is reproduced in a painting of the *Coronation of the Virgin* at the National Gallery called 'Style of Orcagna'. This picture, which formed the high altar of S. Pier Maggiore, shows on the left panel St. Peter kneeling among the adoring saints holding a model of the church (Fig. 6).[9] S. Pier Maggiore was basilican in the style of Arnolfo di Cambio with features which recalled the Badia, Sta. Croce and Sta. Trinita. Flanking the high altar were two chapels on either side, one to the north belonging to the Pazzi and the other three to the Albizzi family who also owned two more chapels on the north aisle.[10]

The Stourhead picture was in the chapel dedicated to S. Niccolò on the south arm of the crossing, next but one to the high altar. This chapel was founded by Orlando degli Albizzi (fl. 1255–d. 1301) who returned from a pilgrimage to Palestine in about 1282 with what were believed to be seven thorns from Christ's crown. He founded the chapel in 1300 and presented the thorns in a reliquary to the Benedictine nuns who, from now on, were obliged to celebrate the feast of S. Niccolò, patron of children and pilgrims. The chapel was originally frescoed with scenes from Orlando's exploits but these frescoes ascribed to Cimabue were, by the seventeenth century, obliterated with whitewash. On one of the pilasters was painted, or hung, a sacred image of St. Ann before which a solemn festival was held annually.[11] St. Ann, the apocryphal mother of the Virgin, appears in *The Protevangelium of James* to have been confused with Hannah (I Samuel i) and hence with barren women bringing forth children miraculously.

Cigoli's altarpiece is signed with the monogram 'CL' and dated '1605'.[12] It is not recorded which member of the Albizzi family commissioned the altarpiece but it was most probably Luca degli Albizzi (1577–1657), last male in direct descent from Orlando, the Chapel's founder. Luca was a courtier, senator, Councillor of State to Ferdinand II de'Medici, owner of the castle of Castelnuovo in

2. Portrait of Cigoli by J. G. and A. Pazzi after G. D. Ferretti's copy of Cigoli's Self Portrait, 1604, in the Uffizi. Line engraving, 25 × 17·6 cm.

Val di Cecina and created in 1638 Marchese di Castelnuovo.[13] Something of a Maecenas, he spent 3,000 scudi on the façade for S. Pier Maggiore designed by Matteo Nigretti in 1637. He was also responsible for recasing Orlando's thorns in a splendid new silver reliquary. In 1597 Luca married Lucrezia de Verrazzano but had no children. His sister Porzia, born in 1586, married a kinsman Giovanni Antonio Cammillo degli Albizzi and in his will Luca left his fortune and estates to her only son who survived infancy, Cammillo degli Albizzi born on 14 January 1609. As Luca's sister married in 1604 it seems likely that the *Adoration of the Kings*, dated 1605, was commissioned as an 'ex voto' by Luca either for her first born child, or for a hoped-for child of his own. That one of these was the reason is especially likely bearing in mind the proximity of the image of St. Ann, the appropriate subject matter of the altarpiece, and the particular importance of an heir to Luca.

Paintings of the *Adoration of the Magi* were rarely

3

3. 'Portrait of Sir Richard Colt Hoare and his Son, by Samuel Woodforde, R.A. (1763–1817), 1795. Canvas, 254 × 168 cm. (National Trust, Stourhead, Wiltshire).

4. **The remaining section of the 17th century façade of S. Pier Maggiore, Florence.**

faithful illustrations of the event described by St. Matthew (2, 1–12) and there is no mention of it in the other three gospels. The Magi's gifts were symbolic; gold for royal power, frankincense for divine majesty, myrrh for human mortality. That the Magi were Kings, three in number symbolizing the Trinity, Three Ages of Man, and the Three Parts of the Known World and were named Caspar, Belthazzar and Melchior came later. Such additions to St. Matthew's account were promoted by the Church, for the homage of earthly kings of all races to Christ the Heavenly King established the divine source of the Church's own authority. Melchior was usually represented as an old man with a long white beard, Caspar as a mature man, and Belthazzar as a young Moor.[14]

The composition of the S. Pier Maggiore altarpiece, which is vertical, depends on the pyramidal groups in the foreground, one formed to the left the Virgin, the Christ Child, St. Joseph and the kneeling Melchior and another to the right formed of Caspar, Belthazzar, a page and two other attendants. These two groups are bound together into a foreground frieze by the sinuous diagonal of Melchior's back which leads the eye up to the Virgin's head. Piercing the composition at the centre, and lighter in key, is a glimpse of the Magi's train and a distant townscape. The event is framed by a building half classical and half rustic. A gloria of *putti* on clouds closes the composition at the top which is broken at the upper centre by the star which shines down through the roof, connecting the upper and lower zones. The spatial organization here is reminiscent of his San Gaggio *Disputation of St. Catherine* (1603), where two vertical masses to the left and right are linked by a kneeling central figure, with *putti* on clouds above,

creating a similar broad unbroken border around the frame's edge, and pierced again at the centre by a distant prospect.[15] In the foreground of the S. Pier Maggiore painting is a large working setter or spaniel which was included as an appealing device to draw the spectator into the action of the picture, forging a link between the physical and the spiritual world.

The palette is generally low-keyed and sombre but, in the foreground, Cigoli makes considerable play with vivid primaries. The Virgin wears crimson and blue silk robes, and St. Joseph a saffron woollen cloak. Melchior, like a Medici, is gorgeously attired in cloth of gold and silver. His robes are lined with ermine, and his left arm is sleeved with purple velvet. Caspar's gown in crimson cut velvet trimmed with spotted leopard, is offset by the blue velvet tunic with slashed sleeves of his page. This youth is most richly dressed, his hem trimmed with pearls and rubies, and, on his feet, violet calfskin boots. He hands his master an

5. **Detail of the façade showing the name of Luca degli Albizzi carved in the frieze.**

6. Detail – 'St. Peter holding a model of the church of S. Pier Maggiore'. From 'The Coronation of the Virgin', Style of Orcagna, 1370–71. Panel c. 29 × 24 cm. (National Gallery, London).

elaborate hexagonal gold lidded casket ornamented with scrolls, foliage festoons and fleur-de-lys. Just visible behind Caspar is the dusky head of Belthazzar wearing a large pearl earring and a gold coronet set with rubies, emeralds, and pearls. A white turban with gold spiked circlet and crimson velvet skull cap has been placed on the ground in the centre foreground and, to the left, stands a rock crystal vase, its brim filled with gold.

As a relief from the chromatic richness of the foreground, the middle distance and distance are loosely and more transparently indicated in a cooler palette of grey, buff, pink and violet. This section of the composition shows a leopard and handler, a helmeted horseman carrying a banner accompanying a turbanned oriental, further horsemen with lances, and, in the background, a giraffe. Over the city walls can be seen a hexagonal centrally planned building surmounted by a shallow dome with a campanile behind it. The sky is a brilliant blue relieved with white scudding clouds, while immediately above in the heavens, lit by the golden light of the star, naked *putti*, with their wings plumed in blue, pink, and green, throw down dog roses, hyacinths and star-of-Bethlehem.

The subject of the altarpiece was evidently given careful thought by the patron and the special form that it was to take considered attentively. The instructions for the commission evidently must have been laid down in considerable detail as Cigoli was in Rome where he had been since the spring of 1604 and was to remain on and off until his death in 1613.[16] The altarpiece is lit partly from the left but mostly from the front as if illumined by the candles on the altar. The Star of Bethlehem, which illumines only the *putti* seated in the clouds, may well have coincided with a natural light source like a high central window. The form of the star is uncommon in that it is eight pointed, rather than six, and is cruciform. This corresponds with the device on the shield of Luca's wife, carved on the façade of S. Pier Maggiore. The Magi process to the left and, in this way, not only venerate the elevated figure of Christ but also indirectly the host on the nearby high altar. The kneeling Melchior does not look at Christ but gazes wrapt, as if receiving the sacrament, at the loose end of Christ's swaddling band. Such a Counter-Reformation demonstration of unworthiness and devotion is a rare variant of the more common portrayal of the Magus kneeling to kiss the Child's toe, while touching the foot only through a thin stole hanging down from the Magus's shoulders.[17] That Melchior is portrayed as if

7. 'Virgin and Child'. Pen and brown ink, blue wash, 14·2 × 10 cm. (Uffizi 1024F recto).

8.   'Adoration of the Magi'. Pen and brown ink, blue wash over traces of lead point 39·5 × 25·3 cm. (Uffizi 982 F).

receiving the sacrament is intentional, for, since the earliest of times, the Incarnation, Christ's appearance on Earth, to which the shepherds and Magi first bore witness, has often been given a eucharistic interpretation.[18]

Cinelli in his *Bellezze . . . di Firenze* particularly admired 'la morbidezza e tenerezza della testa del Santo Re ch'adora il redentore' and drew attention to his act of kissing Christ's extended foot 'con bella attitudine'.[19] In his use of the word 'morbidezza' Cinelli was clearly aware of the typological significance of the event taking place. The action of the King kissing the extended foot of the Christ Child may also anticipate the nailing of Christ's feet to the Cross. This interpretation first appears with Giotto and the Pisani at the end of the thirteenth century and illustrates a passage from *The Meditations of the Pseudo-Bonaventura*.[20] Indeed, the combination of *Crucifixion* and *Adoration* of the Magi occurs comparatively frequently, in fourteenth and fifteenth-century art. This prediction of the Passion would have had added poignancy as, in front of the painting, on the altar table, stood the reliquary containing the seven thorns from Christ's crown. Luca's new casing for the reliquary is probably represented by the offering held by Caspar, as all the preliminary drawings show him holding a model of the church and not this casket. Above Belthazzar's head, driven into a wooden beam, is a large nail. This is a further reference to the Crucifixion and was placed especially above his head because in medieval art the Moorish king foreboded evil: negroes were then often represented playing prominent parts in the defilation and scourging of Christ.[21]

The cavalcade in the background represents the train of the Magi travelling the short distance from Jerusalem to Bethlehem. The train includes a leopard held on a leash: leopards and cheetahs often appear in *Adorations of the Magi* of the International Gothic Style. They have a distinguished Florentine precedent in Gentile da Fabriano's *Adoration of the Magi* in the Uffizi and *The Journey of the Magi* by Gozzoli in the Palazzo Medici-Riccardi. Camels are not included, but the introduction of a giraffe is singular, suggesting that Cigoli may have seen one recently in the Vatican menagerie. In Cigoli's day, although Counter-Reformation churchmen were aware of the many apocryphal aspects of the *Adoration of the Magi*, artists were in no way dissuaded from depicting the subject with all the colourful imagery and symbolism of the Middle Ages.[22]

9. Studio of Cigoli, 'Adoration of the Magi'. Pen and brown ink, blue wash 40·5 × 25·5 cm. (Uffizi 1033F).

10. Detail – 'Two Putti'. From a sheet of studies. Pen and brown ink, blue wash, 12·7 × 12·5 cm. (sheet overall 33·6 × 23·5 cm.) (Uffizi 8958 F).

The drawings that survive for the S. Pier Maggiore altarpiece reveal the artist's inventive processes and working methods. Eight connected drawings are at the Uffizi and two at the Louvre, apart from a 'modello' in oil at Lucca and a reduced replica in a private collection. Probably Cigoli's first thoughts consisted of a series of rapid compositional studies in pen and brown ink scattered across the sheet, like that at the Uffizi for the Pisa *Adoration of the Shepherds* painted three years earlier, but in this case no such studies appear to have survived.[23]

Before starting the S. Piero altarpiece Ludovico Cigoli had made a series of finished studies in pen and brown ink and blue wash, about the size of a playing card, of the Virgin and Child, in some sheets accompanied by St. Joseph and St. John. These, now in the Uffizi, are double sided and are signed on one side with the monogram 'CL'.[24] They were used as a fount for poses in such paintings of the Madonna as those at Budapest and the Pitti. The artist turned to one of this series, *The Virgin seated with the Child on her lap* (Fig. 7), whose pose in reverse recalls Raphael's *Orleans Madonna*.[25] In the S. Piero altarpiece, the pose of the Virgin was reversed, that of the Christ Child retained, and the gesture of the Child's left arm stretching up towards the Virgin's breast, altered to a gesture of benediction. Cigoli commonly reversed images, usually by tracing through from the opposite side of the paper. At an early stage he made a fluent compositional study for the altarpiece in pen and brown ink fortified with blue wash (Fig. 8) which has many differences from the final altarpiece: the composition is reversed; the star is omitted and the *putti* in the heavens are all differently posed.[26] The shapes of the gifts have been changed. Caspar carries one formed like a church, presumably intended to represent S. Pier Maggiore. The dog in the foreground has not yet appeared and there is a different distant background. An intervening autograph sheet, now lost, was then copied by a studio hand with considerable variations especially in the upper zone (Fig. 9) on the reverse of which apparently Cigoli himself lightly traced through the Virgin and the Child, in red chalk, and experimented with an alternative pose for the Child.[27]

On another sheet of studies, in the main probably unconnected with the S. Pier painting (Fig. 10), Cigoli used a corner of the paper to define the poses of two *putti* throwing down flowers that appear on clouds in the upper right of the composition, but the altar piece does not correspond exactly.[28]

At this stage a studio assistant intervened, tracing sections of the earliest compositional sheet (cf. Fig. 8) adding, in a crude hand, architectural variations and superimposing the upper zone in its resolved form, excluding the star (Fig. 11).[29] The subject was now in the same direction as that executed. Next Cigoli studied in greater detail different sections of the composition, working up methodically the principal figures from life. He made a delicate drawing in coloured chalks on blue paper of a small child on his mother's knees, now in the Louvre (Fig. 14). Here the hand positions of the Virgin, as painted, have already been determined, but there is a 'pentimento' to the Child's left arm altering it from its former position of benediction to one of repose. In the same delicate technique he studied the head and shoulders of a bearded old peasant, also in the Louvre (Fig. 13), for the figure of St. Joseph.[30] The old man's sleeveless jerkin was

11. **Studio of Cigoli, 'Adoration of the Magi'. Pen and brown ink, blue wash, 41·2 × 26·3 cm. (Uffizi 983 F).**

12. 'Study for the Virgin'. Black and red chalk heightened with white on blue paper. 19·5 × 17·9 cm. (Uffizi 9659 F).

13. 'Study for St. Joseph'. Black and red chalk heightened with white on blue paper. 25·7 × 17·8 cm. (Louvre Inv. 899).

14. 'Study for the Christ Child'. Black and red chalk heightened with white on blue paper. 25·4 × 10·5 cm. (Louvre Inv. 902).

altered in the altarpiece for the ample folds of a cloak. The Virgin's head, upper torso and left hand were similarly observed from nature in a delicate coloured chalk study on blue paper in the Uffizi (Fig. 12).[31] Here the sitter, without veil, is shown wearing a linen blouse and laced bodice. It has been suggested recently that she was Cigoli's niece, Giovanna Cirula, whose features are also recognizable as the Virgin in the Roti-Michelozzi *Rest on the Flight into Egypt* (*c.* 1607) and, as a foreground figure, in the Pistoia *Birth of the Virgin* (1608).[32] Cigoli made three studies in red chalk on white paper for the drapery around the Virgin's legs (Fig. 15).[33] In this sheet he probably used a posed studio 'garzone'. The figure is not seated on steps, as in the altarpiece, and the arrangement of the draperies is also not as executed. However, it is clear that these studies were intended for the altarpiece as the hands correspond with the Virgin's as painted.

Cigoli turned to blue paper for a drawing, in

15. 'Study for the Virgin's Draperies'. Red chalk 28.5 × 34.4 cm. (Uffizi 8954 F).

black chalk heightened with white, of a bearded nude (Fig. 16) that he used, with modifications to the arm and leg positions, for Caspar.[34] This sheet may first have served for a shepherd to the right in the Pisa *Adoration of the Shepherds* (1602).[35] He also returned to this pose for the figure of Christ in the *St. Peter walking on the Water* at Carrara.[36]

The sequence of drawings is by no means complete lacking many from the life including one for the kneeling Melchior and what would no doubt have been an appealing study for the dog. A highly finished oil 'modello' in the Pinacoteca Nazionale at Lucca adds a little to our knowledge of the painting's development where the main differences are to the retinue of the Magi in the middle distance (Fig. 17).[37] This, or the large replica, in a private collection (Fig. 18), might be identical to a painting referred to by Baldinucci.[38] After de-

scribing the S. Pier Maggiore altarpiece, he recalled that in his youth he saw another painting of the same quality. It included the same dog, and belonged to the Ricasoli family. As no other paintings by Cigoli including a prominent dog appear to be known, it is possible that Baldinucci's youthful memory was at fault and that one of these is the same as the Ricasoli picture.

The altarpiece was most lavishly praised by Cigoli's younger contemporary Baldinucci and remained, as the Florentine guidebooks show, one of the most popular paintings in S. Piero.[39] The composition at once became influential and a challenge to artists like Rosselli, Biliverti, Coccapani and not least the young Carlo Dolci who, in his oil of the *Adoration of the Shepherds* (Fig. 19) now at Cleveland, took the *putti* in the upper right of this composition directly from Cigoli's painting.[40]

Baldinucci drew attention to the English dog 'un cane della bellissima e grande razza di Inghilterra' in the foreground of Cigoli's painting.[41] Apparently the dog was devoted to his master and, when his master died, followed the coffin into the church, eventually to die of a broken heart on his master's tombstone. Colt Hoare certainly knew of this story, quoting it under the description of his painting in *The Modern History of Wiltshire*. The dog may have been one of the reasons why he bought the picture, especially as he had one of a similar breed in England.[42] He secured the picture from a Florentine dealer and painter Giovanni Battista Cassana to whom he paid 300 gold zecchini on 19 February 1791.[43] The picture was then dispatched to Stourhead.

Stourhead, the fine Palladian house built by his great grandfather, was already filled with pictures, and the *Adoration of the Magi* was first hung in the saloon in what must have been very cramped surroundings.[44] Colt Hoare added in 1792–1802 a wing to the north to re-house his collection of pictures, especially those he had recently acquired on his travels: a matching wing was also added to the south to house his large library.[45] These wings, relatively simple and austere, were designed, so to speak, inside out, with the largest element in either building being the Cigoli altarpiece, for which space was allocated at the centre of the west wall of the picture gallery (Fig. 20). Two other masterpieces, previously in the Entrance Hall, were hung to left and right: these were Maratti's *The Marchese Pallavicini conducted by Apollo to the Temple of Fame*, which Colt Hoare's grandfather had bought in 1758, and the pendant, commissioned in 1759, Mengs's *Octavian and Cleopatra*.[46] These three large pictures were lit by three large windows on the opposite wall, with small square windows above serving as substitutes for top-lighting. By this arrangement the pictures dictated the exterior elevation of this and the matching wing to the south (Fig. 21). The Cigoli hung above a marble chimneypiece, carved with a frieze of *The Infant Bacchus conveyed by Mercury to Leucothea*, copied from an antique vase, which Colt Hoare had seen used as a font at Gaeta di Mola.[47] The Cigoli was now the principal picture in a room sumptuously furnished and decorated by Thomas Chippendale the Younger, in a colour scheme of purple, gold stars, yellow and black. A new gilt frame was provided for it, with handsome carved cresting consisting of goat's head, shell, and festoons of oak leaves, for which Chippendale charged ten guineas in 1802.[48] The picture

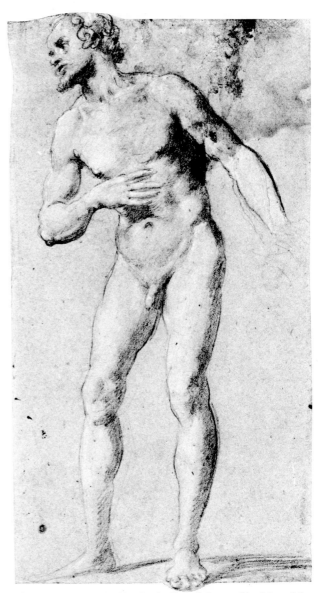

16. 'Male Nude'. Black chalk heightened with white on blue paper, 40·6 × 22·5 cm. (Uffizi 8818F verso).

gallery was clearly in the most advanced Neo-Classical taste, rivalling contemporary interiors by Hope, Soane and Smirke. Sadly, its original colour scheme has been changed to an unadventurous green and white, and Chippendale's upholstery and curtains replaced; nevertheless the paintings mostly remain as Colt Hoare arranged them.

Cigoli's *Adoration*, as we have seen, was painted for a particular person, for a special reason, for a specific destination and as a sacred image in a Florentine church. Now it hangs where it has since the late eighteenth century as the centrepiece of a Neo-Classical interior in an English country house. This altarpiece, placed to advantage in a gallery

17. 'Modello' of the 'Adoration of the Magi'. Canvas, 221 × 147 cm. (Pinacoteca di Lucca). 18. (right) replica—'Adoration of the Magi'. Canvas 156 × 112·5 cm. (Private Collection).

specially designed for it, fulfils aesthetically and spiritually other roles than those originally intended. In its transformed setting Colt Hoare and his contemporaries saw the picture afresh, not just with an antiquarian eye, but for its inherent qualities, the humanity of expression, the nobility of gesture, and the simplicity and directness of the Christian message. They interpreted it in the light of a new and different aesthetic, religious and humanist language, of Reynolds and Flaxman, Lavater and Winkelmann, Wesley and Wilberforce. The picture's role has changed and now forms a landmark in the history of enlightened English taste and connoisseurship during the Romantic period. It is satisfying that Cigoli's *Adoration of the Magi*, a masterpiece of Florentine painting and, by adoption, a vital element of interior decoration, will now remain at Stourhead thanks to the munificence of the Hoare family and the guardianship of the National Trust.

19. 'Adoration of the Shepherds', by Carlo Dolci (1616–1686). Canvas 87·5 × 70 cm. (Cleveland Museum of Art).

20. View of the Picture Gallery, Stourhead, in 1902.

21. East Front of Stourhead. The Picture Gallery, housed in the right wing, was added 1792/3–1802.

Notes

Unless otherwise stated all the drawings and paintings reproduced here are by Cigoli or from his studio. I should like to acknowledge the National Trust, the Trustees of the National Gallery, the Louvre (Cabinet des Dessins) and the Uffizi (Gabinetto Disegni e delle Stampe) for permission to illustrate items in their collections. I should also like to thank my wife Jane for typing this article and making many pertinent suggestions and the following for their most generous assistance: Mlle Roseline Bacou, Mme Sylvie Béguin, Dttssa. Giulietta Chelazzi-Dini, Mr. A. Crookston, Mr. Dudley Dodd, Dr. Michael Evans, Mr. John Gere, Mrs. Judith Goldblatt, Mr. St. John Gore, Mrs. Carmen Gronau, Mr. John Hardy, Mr. Rupert Hodge, Mr. Charles McCorquodale, Dr. Jennifer Montague, Dttssa. Anna Maria Petrioli, Mr. J. Rathbone, Dr. Ruth Rubinstein, Mr. John Sunderland, Mr. Reginald Winder, Mr. Michael Wrench, Mr. Gervase Jackson-Stops, Dttssa. Anna Forlani Tempesti.

[1] St. John Gore, 'Pictures in National Trust Houses', A Supplement to the Burlington Magazine, vol. CXI, April 1969, p. 254. Stourhead with its contents was presented to the National Trust by Sir Henry Hoare, 6th Bart., in 1946. The picture needs cleaning and conservation. The worst damaged area is to the Virgin's right arm. The canvas is torn across her throat and there are further paint losses in the top left corner. A diagonal tear about 80 cms long cuts across the dog's front paws and affects the crystal vase. Some of these damages may have been made good by John Rising, sometime of 85 Portland Street, London, in 1801–2 (see bill, Wiltshire County Record Office, 383/4 Hoare: Household Accounts, p. 160: 'Pictures repaired at Stourhead House/73 revarnished clean'd & repaired . . . £101 9s 6d.')

[2] Apart from specifically Cigoli literature, it is reproduced in: Ellis Waterhouse, Italian Baroque Painting, London, 1962, pp. 151–54, fig. 131; St. John Gore, 'A Worthy Heir to Greatness', Country Life, February 6, 1964, p. 280, fig. 5; C. McCorquodale, 'Aspects of Florentine Baroque Painting', Apollo, September 1974, pp. 198–99, 202, fig. 3.

[3] The essential bibliography is: G. B. Cardi, Vita di Lodovico Cardi Cigoli, San Miniato, 1913, (original Ms. of 1628 in Uffizi, Gabinetto Disegni e delle Stampe); Filippo Baldinucci, Notizie de' Professori del disegno da Cimabue in qua, ed. D. M. Manni, 21 vols., Florence, 1767–74, IX, pp. 32–109; Kurt Busse, Manierismus und Barockstil, ein Entwicklungsproblem der florentinischen Seicentomalerei dargestellt an dem Werk des Lodovico Cardi da Cigoli, Leipzig, 1911; Mario Bucci et al., Mostra del Cigoli, San Miniato, 1959; Giulietta Chelazzi-Dini, 'Aggiunte e precisazioni al Cigoli e alla sua cerchia', Paragone, no. 167, 1963, pp. 51–65; Anna Matteoli, 'Il Cigoli e le Accademie', Commentari, 1973; C. H. Carman, 'A New Painting by Cigoli', Paragone no. 291, 1974, pp. 73–79; Alessandro Gambuti, 'Lodovico Cigoli Architetto', Studi e Documenti di Architettura no. 2, June 1973; Miles Chappell, 'Cigoli's "Resurrection" for the Pitti Palace', Burlington, vol. CXVI, August 1974, pp. 469–74; idem, 'Cigoli's Rest on the Flight into Egypt', Antichità Viva, Anno XIV, no. 4, 1975, pp. 11–16; Charles H. Carman, 'Il "Sacrificio d'Isacco" del Cigoli', Arte Illustrata, no. 59, October 1974, pp. 331–38; idem, 'Cigoli's Annunciation at Montughi: A New Iconography', Art Bulletin, June 1976, pp. 215–24. To this must be added for Cigoli's place in Florentine Art: Walter Friedlander,

[4] Mannerism and Anti-Mannerism in Italian Painting, New York, 1965 ed.

[4] E. Panofsky, 'Galileo as a Critic of the Arts: Aesthetic Attitude and Scientific Thought', Isis, XLVII, 3–15, pp. 182–85.

[5] Sir Richard Colt Hoare, Bart., The Modern History of Wiltshire, vol. 1, London, 1822, p. 79. Colt Hoare was also the author of A Catalogue of Books relating to the History and Topography of Italy, collected in the Years 1786–90, London, 1812; Recollections abroad during the Years 1785–91, 4 vols., Bath, 1815–18; Hints to Travellers in Italy, London, 1815; Classical Tour through Italy and Sicily tending to illustrate some districts which have not been described by Mr. Eustace, London, 1819. For details of Colt Hoare's purchase see note 43.

[6] Walter and Elizabeth Paatz, Die Kirchen von Florenz, Band IV, Frankfurt am Main, 1952, pp. 629–57.

[7] Apart from the Cigoli at Stourhead the most distinguished are the altarpiece with The Coronation of the Virgin, Style of Orcagna, in the National Gallery, The Assumption of the Virgin, school of Botticelli (? Botticini) also in the National Gallery; The Assumption of the Virgin by Francesco Granacci, formerly at Reigate Priory (Paatz op. cit.).

[8] Ristretto di Notizie . . . in Firenze, per Gaetano Cambiagi, Florence, 1789, under 'Aggiunte e Correzioni', p. 94.

[9] No. 569, Martin Davies, The Earlier Italian Schools, National Gallery Catalogues, London, 1961, pp. 389–96. Davies pointed out p. 390: 'It is an iconographical oddity . . . that the Magi are apparently among the groups of adoring saints'. This may be significant for apart from an Adoration of the Magi appearing as one of the panels of this polyptych another Adoration of the Magi was painted either by Rosselli or Pagani in 1605 for the altar flanking the high altar to the north, which was commissioned by Ruberto Antinori. (Christel Thiem, Gregorio Pagani, Stuttgart, 1970, p. 60, G. 51). This painting may be identical to the important altarpiece given to Matteo Rosselli (note by Del Bravo on mount in Witt Library) and now in St. Stephen Walbrook.

[10] Paatz; loc. cit.

[11] Giuseppe Richa, Notizie Istoriche delle Chiese Fiorentine, part I, vol. I, Florence, 1754, p. 137; Follini and Rastrelli, Firenze Antica e Moderna, vol. V, Florence, 1794, pp. 90–91, 97; Count P. Litta, Famiglie celebre Italiane, vol. XI, Turin 1876, p. 168, tav. III.

[12] It is clearly signed in black oil paint in the lower left corner above the dog's left paw. Mario Bucci, following Cardi's Vita (pp. 28 & 52) op. cit., p. 34, gives the date incorrectly as 1601 (and also attributes the façade of S. Pier Maggiore to Cigoli). Paatz following Busse, gives the date as 1603–4, the date also given in Thieme-Becker, VI, 1912, p. 590. Then Paatz, again following Busse, recorded that it was thought to be in the Accademia, Florence.

[13] Litta, op. cit. 1878, tav. XX, XXI.

[14] Louis Réau, Iconographie de l'Art Chrétien, vol. II, part II, Paris, 1957, pp. 236–52 and Jacques de Voragine, La Légende Dorée, (Garnier-Flammarion) Paris, 1967, pp. 114–21.

[15] Bucci, op. cit. pl. LXXXa.

[16] Amongst other commissions in 1605 Cigoli was working on: St. Peter healing the Cripple, ordered by Grand Duke Ferdinando, for St. Peter's; The Investiture of Cosimo I in the order of S. Stefano, for Pisa; an Ecce Homo, in competition with Passignano and Caravaggio, for Monsignor Massimi; a pedestal design for Giambologna's Equestrian statue of

Henri IV, for Paris; the design of the Palazzo Rinuccini, Florence, and the façade of St. Peter's, for Pope Paul V.

17 This action occurs in the Limbourg Brother's rendering *Les Très Riches Heures*, f. 52 r, Chantilly, Musée Condé, and in Botticelli's early *Adoration of the Magi* in the National Gallery (no. 592). For its derivation from Eastern courtly practices as described by Xenophon see: Louis Brétheir, *Les Institutions de l'Empire byzantin*, Paris, 1949. For a general discussion; H. C. Kehrer, *Die heiligen drei Könige in Literatur und Kunst*, Leipzig, 1908.

18 Ursula Nilgen, 'The Epiphany and the Eucharist: On the Interpretation of Eucharistic Motifs in Mediaeval Epiphany Scenes', *Art Bulletin*, XLIX, 1967, pp. 311–16.

19 Giovanni Cinelli, *Le Bellezze della Città di Firenze*, Florence, 1677, pp. 355–56.

20 *Meditationes vitae Christi of Pseudo-Bonaventura* (I. Ragusa and R. B. Green, *Meditations of the Life of Christ*, Princeton, 1961, p. 46ff.).

21 This aspect is to be treated exhaustively in vol. III of the forthcoming Office du Livre publication, *L'Image de Noir*.

22 Emile Male, *L'Art Religieux après le Concile de Trente*, Paris, 1932, pp. 249–52.

23 Compare Uffizi 994 F verso.

24 Other drawings of this group are listed by Chappell in *Antichità Viva*, op. cit. p. 14, no. 3. They were exhibited together in 1913 (P. N. Ferri and F. di Pietro, '*Mostra dei disegni di Lodovico Cardi detto il Cigoli in Gabinetto dei disegni*, Bergamo, 1913, p. 7).

25 This sheet has an unconnected study of the Virgin suckling the Child on the verso.

26 This sheet has an heraldic watermark resembling C. M. Bricquet, *Les Filigranes*, Paris, 1907, p. 139, no. 1884. Bricquet notes that it, and variants, were in use at Lucca, Fabriano, and Rome during the last quarter of the 16th century.

27 Inscribed on verso in black chalk '1033 Sig. Cigoli per la ch. di S. Pier Maggiore'.

28 The drawing is laid down and no watermark is visible. Also on the sheet are studies in black chalk of a man walking forward to the right and, in pen and brown ink, two figures in conversation.

29 The drawing is laid down but architectural drawings are visible through the backing. Inscribed top centre in ink: '28', and bottom left: '855'.

30 Chappell, *Antichità Viva*, op. cit., p. 15, no. 9, draws attention to the use of the same model in other Cigoli compositions.

31 Chappell, *Antichità Viva*, op. cit., pp. 11, 13, 14, no. 4, fig. 3. The author discovered this important Cigoli sheet among the Biliverti drawings at the Uffizi.

32 Chappell, *Antichità Viva*, op. cit., p. 15, no. 9.

33 The drawing is laid down and no watermark is visible.

34 No watermark. Blotches of red and buff wash. Inscribed in an old hand in brown ink lower left: *Del Cigoli*. Another drawing for a figure in an *Adoration* on recto.

35 Bucci, pp. 83–85, no. 31, pl. XXX.

36 The picture was painted for the Church of Riottoli, near Empoli, and a drawing for Christ is in the Staatliche Graphische Sammlung, Munich (inv. 2328). Exhibited: *Italienische Zeichnungen 15–18 Jahrhundert*, Munich 1967, cat. no. 29, pl. 60.

37 The Lucca picture differs from the altarpiece in that (1) a figure behind the standard-bearer to the left is visible and there are two more spears (2) under the arch there is a camel with rider in place of the giraffe (3) the top of the campanile is pointed (4) the *putto* in the sky upper left has both feet visible (5) the bottom point of the star is shorter. The picture is in the Museo Nazionale Villa Guinigi, Lucca (photo sopr. Pisa 1625, as by F. Gessi (1588–1649)).

38 Bought at Sotheby, London, 22 May 1968, lot 51. Reproduced: Chappell, *Antichità Viva*, op. cit., p. 16, fig. 8. (I am most grateful to the owner for allowing me to see this picture and to publish it here.)

39 Cinelli sums this up: '. . . questa in ogni sua parte pregiabile, ed e delle più famose opere che escissero dall'eruditissima mano de si sovrano maestro'.

40 Ann Tzeutschler Lurie, 'Two Devotional Paintings by Sassoferrato and Carlo Dolci', *The Bulletin of the Cleveland Museum of Art*, September 1968.

41 Baldinucci, Follini and Rastrelli, Richa, Bocchi-Cinelli, *loc. cit.*

42 See portrait by Prince Hoare of Sir Richard Colt Hoare's son *Henry Hugh Hoare, later 3rd Bart* (1762–1841), Stourhead no. 138. This shows Henry aged about 20 holding a fowling piece and accompanied by a large spaniel. (Courtauld neg: B60/65).

43 The full text of the bill with the Hoare Papers in the Wiltshire County Record Office, Trowbridge, (vol. 383/4, *Hoare: Household Accounts*, p. 248) reads:

'Ricevuto il di 19 di Febrajo/1791 Tre cento Zecchini in/oro dal Cavaliere Riccardo/Hoare, Inglese per un quadro/vendutogli da me, rappresen/tando l'Adorazione de Re/Magi, opera originale Di/Ludovico Cigoli- quale quadro/prometto di consegnare alle/Mani del Signor Giannini/Pittore Fiorentino-/Giov. Batta. Cassana.

and in Colt Hoare's hand:

'Receipt for a large picture of/the Adoration of Magi by/Ludovico Cigoli- bought by RCH/at Florence- 300 zecchini'.

Colt Hoare in *The Modern History of Wiltshire* (loc. cit.) gave the date of purchase as 1790 which indeed was probably the date of acquisition, payment only being made in February 1791. The item, 1791, 'Feb. 13 To a packing case 18/-' in Sir Richard Colt Hoare's *Personal Account Book 1777–1831* (Archives, Hoare's Bank) may have been for the painting's dispatch to England.

44 Sir Richard Colt Hoare, *A Description of the House and Gardens at Stourhead* . . . . Salisbury and London, 1800, p. 30 (Saloon) no. 133.

45 Kenneth Woodbridge, *Stourhead*, The National Trust Guidebook 1971, pp. 33–36. Christopher Hussey, 'Stourhead', *Country Life*, vol. LXXXIII, 1938, vol. CIX, 1951.

46 For these two pictures see St. John Gore, 'Prince of Georgian Collectors', *Country Life*, Jan. 1964, pp. 210–12.

47 Woodbridge, *op cit*., p. 34.

48 *Bills and Receipts at Stourhead, Wiltshire for Thomas Chippendale the Younger 1795–1820* (photocopy, Victoria and Albert Museum, Woodwork Department) 'Oct. 14 1802, Sundries: Sr Richd Colt Hoare Bart/To Thomas Chippendale.

A Rich Carved ornament for picture frame/of a large Goats head and Oak leaves – £10–10.

For the furnishing of the room, see John Kenworthy-Browne, 'Notes on the furniture by Thomas Chippendale the Younger at Stourhead', *The National Trust Year Book* 1975–76, pp. 93–102.

Lawrence Johnston, Creator of Hidcote Garden

ALVILDE LEES-MILNE

To thousands of gardeners and horticulturists both professional and amateur in Western Europe, and even to some in Australia, the U.S.A., Canada and Africa, the word Hidcote means only one thing. It means one of the most beautiful, interesting, haunting gardens in existence. Yet how many of these thousands of visitors, who go there year after year, ever give a thought to its creator?

Who was Lawrence Johnston? Where did he come from? Why did he choose a remote and cold Cotswold hilltop on which to make this remarkable garden? How, anyway, did he know so much about gardens? In fact, how could any one man in his lifetime create something so perfect? Perhaps it is time he was brought out a little into the limelight which he so much disliked.

Lawrence Waterbury Johnston was born in Paris on 12 October 1871. His father, Elliott Johnston, came from Baltimore, Maryland, U.S.A., and must have died before 1887, for in that year Lawrence's mother, born Gertrude Cleveland, married Charles Francis Winthrop, son of a prominent New York family. Winthrop died in Paris in 1898. The Johnstons, who had Scottish connections, came from the North of Ireland. Lawrence Johnston's early life was spent in France. His parents evidently belonged to that cultured group of rather well-to-do Americans who in the late nineteenth and early twentieth centuries felt drawn to Europe, where they found more to satisfy their interests and where they often settled for good. In fact, they were what are often loosely termed 'Henry James Americans'.

So Lawrence must from an early age have been accustomed to being surrounded by beauty and culture. Walks in the streets of Paris, visits to museums, visits to *châteaux* and *manoirs* with exquisite gardens, all this and a great deal more must have made a lasting impression upon the small boy. Being in a foreign country he was educated at home by a tutor. He was always very close to his mother; when they went to Hidcote, she

lived with him for nearly twenty years and was buried nearby. She seems to have been quite a character, and inevitably somewhat dominated her son.

There is no clear picture to be drawn of him in early years, and there are a great many gaps in our knowledge of his life. When quite young he became a Roman Catholic, possibly through the influence of his French tutor. It is not known when he first came to England, but certainly before he was twenty. The first definite date in his life is 1894 when, after cramming at Shelford, he matriculated at Trinity College, Cambridge. He was then twenty-three. He received an ordinary second class degree in History in 1897, and left the university that year. The next landmark is 1900, when he became a naturalized British subject. In that same year he joined the Imperial Yeomanry as a trooper, and went off to the Boer War. What drew him into that mesh remains a mystery. A longing for adventure perhaps, coupled with a way of seeing a new continent.

In 1902 he returned, and went to live in Northumberland. The reason for this was twofold. Firstly, when in South Africa he made friends with a young man called Savile Clayton, whose home was near Humshaugh. Secondly, he was suffering from weak lungs, and the bracing north country air was considered healthy. In Northumberland he became a student farmer, lodging with a large landowner called Mr. George Ray.

Next comes the important date 1907. Lawrence was then thirty-six years old, and had presumably made up his mind where his real interests lay. It was in this year that his mother, who had now become Mrs. Winthrop, bought for him a property in the heart of the Cotswolds, called Hidcote Bartrim. It consisted of about 280 acres of farmland, a tiny hamlet of thatched cottages, and a small stone farmhouse. There was a wonderful view from the escarpment over the Vale of Evesham away to the

1. **Lawrence Johnston, from a photograph taken in the South of France in the 1930s.**

Malvern Hills. But the great attraction was a huge and ancient cedar of Lebanon and a clump of fine beech trees.

It was a strange choice, as in those days Hidcote was really remote, and one which could only have been made by someone with considerable vision and imagination. There is no doubt that his active interest in farming was a contributory factor to the acquisition of Hidcote. A friend who lives nearby remembers often seeing him ploughing. However, by now gardening had already become his chosen hobby. His interest in and knowledge of horticulture must have grown rapidly. Unfortunately, there are no records to tell us how he planned the garden at Hidcote. Luckily Mrs. Winthrop had a considerable fortune to draw on, and her son knew how best to spend it.

A wing for Mrs. Winthrop was added to the little farmhouse, today known as the Manor, and other parts of the house were structurally altered with various embellishments. The farmyard was turned into a respectable courtyard and the cottages were renovated. Later Lawrence designed and built one or two more. He also converted a small barn in the courtyard into a chapel where sometimes he would have Low Mass said, or what the French call a 'messe de chasse'.

Life in the country must have been very agreeable in those pre-Great War years, and from this point of view Hidcote was in an auspicious situation geographically. A few miles away at the foot of the escarpment lay Broadway. This lovely little town, as yet undiscovered by tourists, was in its intellectual heyday. A beautiful and famous American actress, Mary Anderson, had come to live there with her Spanish husband, Antonio de Navarro. They had a wide circle of interesting friends. Amongst others, Elgar, Sargent, William Morris and Burne-Jones were frequent visitors. The Navarros, too, were planning and planting a garden which today is of considerable interest and beauty. Writing in 1936 in her book *A Few More Memories*, Madame de Navarro said: 'My Italian friends regard Hidcote as the most beautiful garden they have seen in England. Its wonderful blending of colours and its somewhat formal architectural character please them particularly.' Later she wrote of seeing Reginald Farrer's incomparable gentian blooming at Hidcote in November. 'It seemed too good to be true.' But of course this was sixteen years later.

Most of Lawrence Johnston's friends were passionate and knowledgeable gardeners. Here again he was fortunate in having several in the vicinity – Major Mark Fenwick at Abbotswood, the great alpine grower Clarence Elliot near Moreton-in-Marsh, Lord Barrington then living at Armscote and later at Nether Lypiatt, where he emulated the tapestry hedges at Hidcote, and George Lees-Milne at Wickhamford. Later the Jack Muirs came to Kiftsgate, which is at the end of the Hidcote drive. Here they created a garden which was to become a rival to Hidcote, though entirely different in character, and which to this day is still very spectacular, and of course immortalized by the great climbing rose that bears its name. Mrs. Muir and Lawrence Johnston were able to help each other, and enjoyed many years of close gardening partnership. Then there was Norah Lindsay. Mrs. Lindsay was probably Lawrence Johnston's closest woman friend, and though she did not live nearby, was a constant visitor. She herself was no mean garden architect, and amongst her achievements is the parterre which she re-designed on the south side of Blickling Hall in Norfolk. She was gay, witty, amusing, and indeed wonderfully stimulating. Another, geographically distant, friend was 'Bobbie'

2. A vista in the garden at Hidcote.

3. **The avenue of Huntingdon elms at Hidcote in 1960 now destroyed by elm disease.**

James (The Hon. Robert James), creator of that lovely garden St. Nicholas, near Richmond, Yorkshire, and like Lawrence Johnston, an avid collector of rare plants. In fact his friends were legion, each perhaps contributing an idea here and there towards the eventual form of the Hidcote which we know today.

Little by little the garden grew, and the acres of rough pasture were turned into acres of botanical and horticultural interest. Lawrence Johnston's planting was entirely original. It was the very opposite of the conventional herbaceous border setting, so popular among his contemporaries. His blending of sophistication and simplicity was unique. Nowhere else, except perhaps at Sissinghurst, are unusual plants found growing in cottage garden-like settings. This unusual conception of little gardens within a large garden was entirely novel, as were the tapestry hedges and many other schemes.

I have been told that a trainful of lime-free soil arrived from Surrey for the camellias, rhododendrons and other lime-hating plants. This was mixed with rotted sawdust and peat. Those extraordinary lines of hornbeams, looking like hedges on stilts, appeared later, as did the two little brick and stone pavilions with their pointed, ogival roofs, each side of the centre walk. They are said to be copied from something Lawrence Johnston saw in France. But who knows? Some think they have a Dutch influence. The great avenue of Huntingdon elms by the north approach, now sadly devastated by the catastrophic elm disease, was a piece of truly bold planting, as was the holly avenue leading to the courtyard entrance. One could cover pages eulo-

gizing the endless and enthralling innovations at Hidcote, but that is not the purpose of this article. Many people have described the garden, but perhaps no one better than Vita Sackville-West in an article for the *Royal Horticultural Society Journal* of November 1949. Anyone who has read it can be left in no doubt as to the genius of Lawrence Johnston. The truth is that in spite of, or because of, its simplicity and bold planting Hidcote has a sophisticated, continental flavour, which in a way puts one in mind of gardens in the Isle-de-France.

Like all dedicated gardeners Johnston was both acquisitive and generous. Yet he allowed no room for poor specimens and failures. He believed in cramming his beds and borders with what he most wanted so that there was less space for what he did not want, i.e. weeds. People began to send him

4. **The Stilt Garden at Hidcote.**

5. **Clipped yews in the Pillar Garden.**

plants from far and wide, and as his knowledge grew, so did his collection.

In his day there was a large winter plant house for the more tender things, a place for the cultivation of lush, sub-tropical species of rare plants, which he had collected on his travels or had been sent by other connoisseurs. Unfortunately, when the National Trust took over the garden, this house, proving too costly to run, was demolished and the collection dispersed.

For seven quiet years the garden grew, and Lawrence Johnston worked alongside his gardeners. For he was no onlooker. He dug, and planted, and pruned as much as they did. Then came 1914 and the Great War. All thoughts of gardening were now laid aside. Lawrence Johnston, who had never

6. The Manor House, seen above the Lily Pond.

retired from the Army, was promoted a Major and immediately sent off to France. Owing to his friendship with Savile Clayton, his commission was in the Northumberland Fusiliers. Nothing much is known about his military career except that he was wounded at the very beginning of the War, and again later. At one point he was laid out with a lot of other bodies awaiting burial. By chance an old friend from Broadway, Colonel Henry Sidney, had

been detailed to see to the burial ceremony, and as he passed Major Johnston, he not only recognized him but saw him move.

When Johnston returned from the War there was much to be done at Hidcote. Four years' neglect in a garden can alter it drastically. As things gradually returned to normal he began to think of going off plant collecting, and in 1927 and 1931 he undertook two enthralling expeditions. The first was with

7. One of the twin gazebos, designed by Lawrence Johnston.

8. **The long walk, with clipped hornbeam hedges.**

Major Collingwood (Cherry) Ingram on a four-months trip from Cape Town to the Victoria Falls, during which time he climbed the Drakensburg Mountains. George Taylor (later Sir George Taylor and Director of Kew Gardens) and Reginald Cory made up the party. The expedition has been splendidly recorded by Major Ingram in his book, *A Garden of Memories*. Lawrence Johnston, who liked his comforts, brought along his Italian cook and chauffeur valet. Major Ingram describes Johnston as a typical bachelor, wholly dedicated to gardening, and says that of the four of them he was by far the most catholic in his choice of plants. He would collect members of any genus if they had the slightest claim to beauty. The result was a vast accumulation of living material which he sent for the most part to Edinburgh Botanic Gardens. Many of these plants were later to go to Mentone where he had acquired a property and was making

another garden. The second expedition was much longer, more remote and tougher. Johnston accompanied George Forrest on what was to be Forrest's last journey to Yunnan in China. But unfortunately he fell ill and had to come home before the expedition was completed. Amongst other plants which he brought back was that lovely, tender creeper, *Jasminum polyanthum*, which he grew in his South of France garden. Later he gave a plant of it to Major Warre at the Villa Roquebrune, who in 1938 sent a cutting to England. The *Botanical Magazine* featured it in an article that year. Although it was already known to Kew from seeds which Forrest had collected in 1925 this was its first published reference, and from then on every plant-lover wanted it. Major Johnston also collected the seeds of *Mahonia siamensis*, and *Mahonia lomarifolia*. The former is tender. It grew very well in his Mentone garden where, just before his death in 1958, it was still looking superb. He also gave it to Cambridge Botanic Gardens. *Mahonia lomarifolia* is less tender and does well in sheltered positions in this country. It is a spectacular plant with its whorls of golden flowers in the winter. It is thought that amongst other species the seeds of *Hypericum hidcote* may also have been collected by him, but this is uncertain. Major Johnston also made several less adventurous journeys in pursuit of rarities for his gardens. The list of plants sent from his Mentone garden to the Cambridge Botanic Garden after his death is staggering. Unfortunately, few have survived.

He bought the Serre de la Madone, as his French property was called, in the early twenties, with a view to creating a garden which he might enjoy in the winter months. It lies in one of the hidden valleys running up behind Mentone to the foothills of the Alpes Maritimes, right on the Italian frontier. It is a perfect natural setting for a sub-tropical garden, and was already well planted with olive and citrus trees, and sheltered from every wind. Major Johnston became increasingly absorbed in this Mediterranean paradise, which he crammed with all the plants that would not grow in the cold Cotswolds. He had many gardening friends along the Riviera. Mrs. Warre and her husband lived nearby at the Villa Roquebrune. They shared his tastes and had also created a magnificent garden on terraces overhanging the Mediterranean. Today it is almost the only great pre-war garden left.

Much further west at Hyères lived in those days that renowned French gardener, the Vicomte de Noailles. His property adjoined that of another of Major Johnston's close friends, Edith Wharton. He often visited them both. Mrs. Wharton, writing to Louis Bromfield in 1935, asked, 'Do you know a Spanish rose called Apelles Mestres? Lawrence Johnston tells me it is the most beautiful rose in the world.' And again later she wrote for the address of a nurseryman near Mortefontaine, 'where we all went one day last summer, and Lawrence Johnston who was staying with me, very kindly ordered for me a very big and splendid magnolia, to be "mis en bac" and delivered in the spring. Neither he nor I seem to have noted the address, and Johnnie wants to be sure the "mis en bac" has been done.'

With the Vicomte de Noailles he planned a journey to Burma for 1938 but owing to the menace of another World War it never took place. The Noailles had a squash court and Major Johnston spent many hours playing in it. He was also a keen tennis player and liked to get profes-sionals to come and play with him both at Hidcote and in France. He was at the Serre de la Madone when the Germans invaded France, and was evacuated on that terrifyingly overcrowded ship which brought thousands of stranded Britons home in 1940.

During the War he remained at Hidcote, struggling to keep things going, and had some Americans billeted on him. Later his memory began to fail and he found the effort of managing the garden increasingly difficult. Also, he wanted to make suitable arrangements for its preservation after his death. An old friend, Lady Colefax, persuaded him he could not do better than give it to the National Trust. After many months of negotiation the deeds were finally signed, and in 1948 Hidcote Bartrim Garden became the first property the Trust was to acquire under the new gardens scheme. Major Johnston retained the use of the house for his life. Partly for tax and partly for climatic reasons he planned to spend most of the year in France, with three months at Hidcote. Although the arrangement was a great weight off his mind, it was a sad one for, as he remarked to an old friend, 'Hidcote is not my baby any more.'

Norah Lindsay died but her daughter Nancy, herself a keen plantswoman, adopted Johnnie, as his friends called him, giving everyone to under-stand that she was his 'seeing eye', and that she knew just what his wishes were. This assumption led to difficulties, and in 1949 the Trust decided to form a small committee of his local friends, capable of managing the garden in his absence. It consisted of Colonel Shennan, who was the chairman and whose son was Major Johnston's godson, Mrs. Muir from Kiftsgate, Mr. de Navarro, the son of Mary Anderson de Navarro, who had inherited his parents' house in Broadway, and inevitably Miss Lindsay. At that time there were four gardeners. Three of them received £4 a week, and Hawkins the head gardener £4 10s. until he asked for a rise, and got £5. In 1949 Hawkins exhibited some geraniums at the Chelsea Flower Show and won the Banksian Medal. In those early days of opening to the public, attendance was very small. The garden was open for one shilling from 2 till 5 p.m. on three days a week. On an August afternoon in 1949 someone counted seven visitors. In June 1950 the admission charge was raised to 1s. 6d and it was thought very splendid that one day in May a hundred people came. The story is very different today. In 1976 there were approximately 60,000 visitors.

9. The garden at La Serre de la Madone near Mentone, created by Lawrence Johnston in the 1920s.

10. The villa and terraces at La Serre de la Madone.

What more do we know about the creator of this truly great and unique garden? He was a small man with fair hair and very blue eyes. One of his old friends described him as blithe. He was shy and modest. He was scrupulous. When visiting the Vatican garden on one occasion he could not resist picking a piece of water ranunculus. Whereupon, turning to a friend he said, 'Excuse me, I must now go and light a candle.' He also hated publicity. Of the many plants for which we are indebted to him today only one or two bear his name, but many that of Hidcote. He endeared himself to all who knew him well, especially his staff. He had natural good taste in everything from gardening to arranging his house. He was an avid reader of all horticultural literature, and his library contained a fine collection of books on this subject. He enjoyed painting and did a frieze for one of the rooms at Hidcote, as well as decorating the two little garden pavilions. He also decorated a room in the Florentine style for the Muirs at Kiftsgate. He collected old glazed tiles on his travels, which he used very effectively in the bathrooms, kitchens and garden rooms of his two houses. He had a number of French eighteenth-century lead watering-cans, which he would group in strategic corners of his gardens. His choice of garden furniture was faultless and included some lovely reeded iron seats and fine terracotta urns. Some of these were regrettably dispersed among other National Trust gardens. He was inseparable from his pack of little dachshunds who went with him to France when he finally decided to leave England. He never married. Above all he loved his gardens. He died at the Serre de la Madone in 1958, and is buried beside his mother in Mickleton churchyard, a mile or two from his beloved Hidcote.

Over his grave we read:-

Lawrence Waterbury Johnston, son of Elliot Johnston and Gertrude Cleveland Winthrop. Born 12 October 1871. Died 27 April 1958. Deeply loved by all his friends.

R. J. Wyatt's 'Flora and Zephyr' at Nostell Priory

JOHN MARTIN ROBINSON

Standing in a corner of the Tapestry Room at Nostell Priory in Yorkshire is one of the finest works of English neo-classical sculpture, the *Flora and Zephyr* of R. J. Wyatt (Fig. 1). Its presence in an Adam room cheek by jowl with Flemish tapestries and Chippendale furniture is slightly incongruous and poses an unexplained problem of provenance. Until recently not even the subject was known and the group was mistakenly described as *Cupid and Psyche*. Nor is it certain when it was brought to Nostell. Probably it was acquired by Charles Winn who inherited in 1817 and subsequently collected many of the pictures and *objets d'art* now in the house, but there is nothing in the Nostell archives to prove this.

R. J. Wyatt was originally commissioned to carve this subject by the 1st Lord Wenlock for Escrick Park in Yorkshire. He received £400 for it.[1] The finished work was exhibited at the Royal Academy in 1834 where it was an object of general admiration. Lord Wenlock, however, died before the statue was completed and, though paid for, it may not have found its way to Escrick. The present owner of Escrick has no memory of it ever having been there and it is not among the surviving nineteenth century sculpture in the collection.[2]

It is possible, therefore, that the statue at Nostell could be the original version made for Lord Wenlock and acquired by Charles Winn after his death. On the other hand it may be a replica, for R. J. Wyatt made replicas of nearly all his works, sometimes providing as many as six copies of a popular subject. He is known to have made a replica of the *Flora and Zephyr* for Lord Otho FitzGerald, so it is quite possible that he made one for Charles Winn as well.[3]

Whatever its provenance, there is no doubt about the quality of the group. It is one of R. J. Wyatt's best early works, executed when he was still strongly under the influence of Canova. It is among the first of a series of groups and individual figures which were extremely popular with English aristocratic collectors and most of which were exhibited at the Royal Academy, despite the fact that Wyatt had no very high opinion of the way sculpture was displayed there.

He expressed his views in a forthright letter to his friend John Gibson:

The impression which the Sculpture Room made on me at first was most disagreeable and had more the appearance of a brokers' shop than works arranged for exhibition, your two bas reliefs were placed opposite the window consequently they had no effect of light and shade whatever and all the delicate modelling of the parts was lost, you would have been annoyed had you seen them so placed for they looked very different in your studio when properly lighted, my two statues had a central situation but were both stuck close to a miserable statue of the queen so that the stools on which the three statues were placed formed one pedestal and therefore some of the best views of each of my statues were impossible to be seen, the statues had been pawed over and were dirty and altogether looked very different from what I would have wished'.[4]

R. J. Wyatt is now almost forgotten, but he was the greatest English sculptor of the second quarter of the nineteenth century and in his lifetime he enjoyed an international reputation. He was the fourth son of Edward Wyatt, a carver, gilder and picture-frame maker, and was born over his father's shop in Oxford Street on 3 May 1795. As a youth he worked for his father and early decided to be a sculptor. He was apprenticed at the age of fourteen to J. C. F. Rossi. In 1812 he entered the Royal Academy Schools and three years later won the Academy's silver medal for the best drawing from life. Rossi gave him a good practical groundwork in his art. While with him he carved some marble chimney-pieces and simple memorial tablets, the stock in trade of the eighteenth and early nineteenth century English sculptor.[5]

1. 'Flora and Zephyr' by R. J. Wyatt, 1834. (Collection Lord St. Oswald, Nostell Priory, Yorkshire.)

2. 'Cupid and Psyche', by Antonio Canova, 1797 (Paris, the Louvre).

3. 'Flora', by R. J. Wyatt, 1841. Replica for Sir Arthur Brooke (formerly at Colebrooke, Co. Fermanagh).

His ambition, however, was to be a sculptor of life-size allegorical and mythological subjects. In 1818 he exhibited his first attempt, a *Judgement of Paris*, at the Royal Academy. He determined to go to Rome to complete his training under the great Canova himself. Sir Thomas Lawrence, who was impressed by Wyatt's work, is reputed to have introduced him to Canova when the latter visited England. Canova promised Wyatt his protection and permission to work in his studio should he go to Italy. Wyatt took advantage of this invitation and left England in 1820. He made his way to Rome via Paris, where he spent some time in the studio of the distinguished sculptor Baron François-Joseph Bosio.[6]

He arrived in Rome early in 1821 and received the promised place under Canova's tutelage. There he met another young expatriate sculptor, John Gibson, who had already been in Italy for two years. They became life-long friends. On Canova's death a year later they both transferred to Thorwaldsen's studio before setting up on their own in studios opposite each other in the Via Fontanella Barberini. Though Wyatt was lucky enough to receive an order for the *Musidora*, now at Chatsworth, from the Duke of Devonshire, his first few years on his own were not a success. He was neglected for a time and received no further commissions until about 1829 when a visitor to Rome noted a number of statues in his studio for English clients.[7]

Once he had gained recognition, however, he rapidly became one of the most popular and sought-after sculptors of the age. From 1830 until his premature death twenty years later in 1850, he was loaded with commissions from distinguished

English and foreign patrons including Queen Victoria, the King of Naples, the Duke of Leuchtenberg, a Russian Grand Duke and the English Prime Minister, Sir Robert Peel. Lord Wenlock, who commissioned the *Flora and Zephyr*, also commissioned a bust of his wife and a group of his two sons dressed as hunters.

The last years of Wyatt's life in Rome were overcast by political disturbances. During the 1848 rebellion there was considerable xenophobic feeling among the Roman population. As a result he was forced to give up his studio in the Via Fontanella and to look for a new one, though he never moved there. When the French bombarded the city, he very narrowly escaped with his life. One of the shots exploded in his studio just after he had entered. He wrote to Gibson (who had fled from the city to the Baths of Lucca) to describe his 'miraculous escape' and how he had picked up nine pieces of the shell from the floor afterwards. Some of his plaster casts were destroyed, while others were damaged.[8]

These various traumas affected his health and he died a year later on 27 May 1850, after a short illness. His cleaning woman discovered him early one morning lying on the floor 'speechless and

4. **Detail of 'Flora'.**

gasping his last'. He was buried in the English Cemetery and his funeral was attended by nearly fifty artists and friends. Gibson carved his tombstone with a medallion portrait and a resounding epitaph: 'His works were universally admired for their purity of taste, grace and truth of nature. The productions of his genius adorn the Royal Palaces of England, St. Petersburg and Naples as well as the residences of the nobility and gentry of his own country'.[9]

Throughout the twenty years of his success he specialized almost entirely in life-size statues. Unlike contemporaries in England, such as Sir Francis Chantrey, he carved remarkably few church monuments or portrait busts. Also unlike many of his contemporaries, he eschewed the overtly sentimental and the dramatically naturalistic and remained true to the standards of Thorwaldsen and Canova to the end.

This is apparent in the Nostell *Flora and Zephyr*. It is clearly based on Canova's group of *Cupid and Psyche* (1797), now in the Louvre (Fig. 2). The comparatively early date of this group in Wyatt's development is shown by a slight weakness of composition such as is not apparent in his later work. The two figures are not properly integrated to form a single unified whole. Contemporary critics felt that the group was mainly a statue of Flora, with the Zephyr as an unrelated appendage. Wyatt later reproduced the Flora as a single statue for Sir Arthur Brooke and exhibited it at the Royal Academy in 1841 (Figs. 3 and 4); this reinforces the view that the Nostell group is not a fully integrated composition.

This reservation apart, the work is of great beauty. One of the most striking features of Wyatt's statues is their excellent finish. He paid more attention to this than any of his contemporaries and always finished his statues himself. This contrasts with Gibson, for instance, who, as he achieved greater success, left more and more of the marblework to assistants.

In the first place, Wyatt took great pains to select marble of high quality for his work. An example of this is the *Infant Bacchus* exhibited at the Royal Academy in 1848. He described the marble as 'most beautiful, being of that warm tint which is so favourable to sculpture'.[10] He did his utmost to give his work a warm soft quality which is far more agreeable than the cold harshness of much neoclassical sculpture. It is probable that he learnt this technique from Bosio, many of whose statues are like satin. Dr. Waagen noticed this particular quality of Wyatt's work when he praised its 'soft delicate execution'.[11]

Wyatt's carving also shows great concern for contrasts in texture and finish. In the *Flora and Zephyr* the different surfaces, flesh, hair, flowers, wings, drapery and the bark of the tree, are all beautifully handled. This concern for texture, however, is not carried to the point of excessive naturalism.

Restraint and balance is the keynote of the group. It avoids the obvious emotion and sentimentality which such a subject might have incurred from a lesser artist. Flora's expression is one of chaste calm and introspection, neither mawkish nor titillating as are so many Victorian statues of female nudes. Contemporaries considered this absence of emotion a fault, but to us it appears one of the greatest strengths of his work.[12]

The *Flora and Zephyr* at Nostell is a fine example of the work of a sculptor who has been sadly undervalued. R. J. Wyatt was an artist of great sensitivity and technical accomplishment, who was considered at the time to have 'surpassed all living artists in representing the pure and delicate beauty of the female form'.[13]

Notes

I am most grateful to Lord St. Oswald for permission to write this article, to Major T. Ingram for checking the Nostell archives for me, to Mr. John Kenworthy-Browne for helpful advice, and to Mrs. Rosemary Warburton for allowing me to make use of her unpublished Leeds University M.A. thesis on R. J. Wyatt.

[1] Northumberland Record Office: Ridley MSS. ZRI 33/5, R. J. Wyatt to Sir Matthew Ridley, 25 June 1834.

[2] The neo-classical sculpture from Escrick now belongs to Lord Wenlock's descendant, Mr. Nigel Forbes Adam of Skipwith Hall, Yorkshire.

[3] Lord Otho FitzGerald's *Flora and Zephyr* was sold at Christie's, 10 May 1884.

[4] R.A. MSS. G1/364, R. J. Wyatt to John Gibson, 9 August 1841.

[5] *Art Journal*, 1850, p. 249.

[6] R. Gunnis, *Dictionary of British Sculptors*, 1951, p. 448.

[7] *Literary Gazette*, 1829, p. 476.

[8] R. A. MSS. G/1/365, R. J. Wyatt to John Gibson, 3 July 1849.

[9] *Art Journal*, 1850, p. 249; *Gentleman's Magazine*, 1850, II, p. 99.

[10] Birmingham Reference Library, Galton 390, R. J. Wyatt to J. H. Galton, 15 February 1848.

[11] G. F. Waagen, *Treasures of Art in Great Britain*, 3 volumes, 1854.

[12] *Art Journal*, 1849, p. 176.

[13] *Gentleman's Magazine*, II, 1850, p. 99.

Housekeeping in the Eighteenth and Nineteenth Centuries

KARIN-M.WALTON

The upkeep of a medium- or large-sized English country house before 1900 was a considerable undertaking, especially if the house was in continual use, and it provided full-time occupation for the indoor staff. The task of keeping the house and its contents presentable fell largely to the housekeeper and housemaids. The housekeeper was the senior female servant and one of the 'upper' servants who dined apart from the rest. She was generally middle-aged and had had some experience in lesser posts so that she thoroughly understood the workings of a household. Her responsibilities included superintending the household and, in particular, the female servants, caring for the linen and stores, making preserves and distilling cosmetic and medicinal preparations; for all this she could expect to earn between twenty-five and fifty guineas per annum in 1825.[1] With regard to the housework, her role was mainly supervisory and it was the housemaids who performed the actual chores.

Eighteenth-century households seem to have managed with a minimum number of maids. During the 1760s, Knole, Kent, was run with two housemaids out of a total staff of thirteen which included at least two estate workers.[2] However, demarcation lines were not strictly applied and help would have been forthcoming from the kitchen- and laundry-maids. At Petworth House, West Sussex, the establishment in 1717–18 numbered twelve men, at least eight of whom worked outside, and six women including the housekeeper, two housemaids and a laundry-maid.[3] Petworth was only one of the Duke of Somerset's properties; at Syon and his London house he employed a further forty servants, some of whom would doubtless have travelled from house to house with the family. This probably explains why, in 1769, a list of servants at Petworth numbered only eight, and of these only two worked indoors.[4] The vast armies of servants associated with country houses were mainly a Victorian and Edwardian phenomenon; by 1880, the domestic staff at Petworth had risen to thirty-four, including eight housemaids.[5]

The housemaid was an 'under' servant and, as such, dined either in the servants' hall or, in some places, in the kitchen, segregated from the men. Her life was regulated by rules. In one household the maids had to be up early and in bed by eleven, with half-an-hour for breakfast and an hour for dinner. They had to ask permission to go out, but this was to be granted, 'when asked with discretion & at times not inconvenient'. Regular church-going was obligatory, and 'indecent behaviour' and 'juncketting' were not tolerated.[6] Allowances of food, soap and candles were strictly decreed. At Mellerstain, Berwickshire, the servants' menu varied little:

Sunday they have boild beef and broth . . .
Monday broth made on Sunday and a Herring
Tuesday broth and Beef
Wednesday broth and 2 egs each
Thursday Broth and beef
Fryday Broth and Herring
Saterday broth without meat, and cheese, or a puden, or blood pudens, or a hagish, or what is most convenient.

In addition, there was bread and beer with each meal.[7]

Many mistresses concerned themselves with the welfare of their servants. The letters of the Verney ladies of Claydon House, Buckinghamshire, show that they took a personal interest when servants were ill, but such kindness was not always reciprocated and the family had its share of problems. In 1710, Lady Fermanagh wrote in desperation to her husband:

The Keeper is such a dredfull fellow that for my part I can't immagin what the maids will doe with him, for he went in the Beer Seller and he is more drunk than yesterday . . . & because the Cooke lock'd the

1. Jane Ebbrell, housekeeper at Erddig, North Wales aged 87 in 1793. From a series of portraits in the Servants' Hall.

Seller Doore in the afternoon, as I order'd her . . . he nail'd up all the Larders & the Cook's Chamber doore . . . & the gardener is as bad.

Indoor servants could behave even worse, as Ralph Verney reported to his father:

My butler has behaved very saucily to Mrs Verney upon which I gave him warning to leave me the day before yesterday.[8]

The housemaid's annual wages rose slowly from £3 at Knole in 1662/3 to a recommended £28 in 1915.[9] In the second half of the eighteenth century, an upper housemaid could expect between £8 and £10, excluding her board-wages which were allowed at around six shillings per week, and beer money. In 1865, Jane Carlyle offered a prospective housemaid, 'twelve pounds a year and one pound ten for beer money which she may drink or save – as she likes'.[10] There were occasional additions to a maid's wages in the form of tips or 'vails' from house guests. At Knole these were added together and shared out annually; in 1763, £79.16s. was divided between twenty-five servants, the two housemaids each receiving £3.[11] Legacies were another source of money; when the Earl of Egremont died in the same year, a total of £307.4s. was divided between fifteen servants at Petworth, the housemaid receiving £14 which was equivalent to two years' wages.[12]

Maids usually slept in the attics, in rooms often eccentrically furnished with items relegated from the main rooms. The contents of the laundry maids' room at Dyrham Park, Avon, were typical:

A Press Bedstead a feather bed bols[r] 3 Blankets & 2 ruggs a table bedstead 4 Blankets a flock bed bols[r] & Pillow a rugg 2 Chairs a stoole & a Large Chest some Chair Cases 3 stoole Cushions & some flannell Hangings.[13]

The social highlight of the servants' year was the Servants' Ball, traditionally held around Christmas. Jane Carlyle reported on one such affair at The Grange, Hampshire:

The day after Christmas there was a Grand Ball for

2. **Mrs. Smith, the housekeeper; Thomas (known as 'Tompy'), Mrs. Percy Wyndham's maid, who married Owen, valet to the 1st Lord Leconfield; and Mr. Dine the butler. From an album of photographs of 'all the dear Servants at Petworth', taken by Mrs. Percy Wyndham between 1860 and 1869.**

3. **An attic bedroom at Erddig, showing a maid's 'Press Bedstead' with angled tester to fit under the slope of the roof.**

the servants and their friends – but of that we saw nothing – only heard the music and the carriages 'putting down'! Four maids came from Stratham . . . in their white muslin dresses, with broad sashes of white silk coupe and large (?) silver pins in their hair. They danced the creatures from eight in the evening till six of the morning and the housemaids went straight from dancing to cleaning the grates![14]

The housemaid's duties depended on the size of the house and on what other staff were kept. Where there were both housemaids and chamber-maids, the latter looked after the bedrooms while the housemaids took care of the rest of the house, excepting the kitchen area which was the province of the kitchen-maid. Parlour-maids were a nine-teenth-century innovation and had responsibility for the dining-room.

In general, a housemaid in a large establishment led a tolerable life. Less fortunate, often, was the single maid servant employed by countless middle-class families, who was expected to combine the roles of housemaid, kitchen-maid and footman. Such a servant was required by Jane Carlyle. Writing to a prospective maid in 1865, by which

time she also employed a cook, she listed what was expected of her maid:

> What my Housemaid has to do, is just I suppose what other Housemaids have to do, where there are only two Servants kept. She has to do the Housework, to answer the door, to wait at table, to be the least bit of Lady's maid to me, and the least bit of valet to Mr. Carlyle. As the house is of moderate size, and as we have no dinner-parties and as both Mr. C. and myself are *orderly*, the work is certainly not heavy for any one who understands her business.[15]

Daunting though these demands might seem, they applied equally in thousands of other households and were not to blame for the Carlyles' servant problem, vividly described elsewhere.[16] Maids did tend to leave their posts after a few years, either to marry or to 'better' themselves, but the Carlyles' record of thirty-four maids in thirty-two years was not typical.

The amount of help afforded the maids by the men servants varied. In the eighteenth century, footmen brought in firewood and helped with heavy work, such as turning the mangle. By the early nineteenth century it was accepted that the footmen helped with cleaning furniture and brass, but later in the century, the footman's role became more ceremonial.

The housemaid's routine was handed down by word of mouth and later enshrined in various manuals.[17] The first essential was to rise early, between five and six, although an extra half-hour in bed was allowed during winter months, not out of compassion but to save candles and coal. She began by opening the shutters in the downstairs rooms and then started work on the fires, first removing any hearth rugs and pulling back or covering the carpet with a dust sheet. The ashes were cleared into a metal pail and the grate swept. Fire-irons were of two types. The 'common' type was cleaned with vinegar and ash and polished with an oily rag and brick-dust. Steel irons were cleaned with oil and emery powder in the eighteenth century, although Mrs. Beeton advised against the use of the latter except on the grate bars; rubbing with a dry leather was less damaging. The fire could now be lit and the marble surrounds wiped with soapy water. Stone hearths were scoured with cold water, soap and sand, but tiled areas, warned Hannah Glasse, should be wiped gently, 'for too much rubbing and scrubbing only loosens the Tiles'.

In summer, when there were no fires, the procedure was modified. There were several ways of preserving the irons from rust without having to clean them every day; they could be polished with camphor and hog's lard, or rubbed with goose grease and wrapped in paper until winter. Mrs. Beeton mentions the practice of having two sets of fire bars, a black set for use and a polished set for summer.

When the fires were finished, the brass door-fittings were cleaned. If lacquered, they were simply rubbed with a dry leather; otherwise they were polished with an oily rag and rotten-stone or brick-dust. To protect the door, a piece of card with a hole cut in it was slipped round the handle.

Before beginning on the floor, the windows and shutters were dusted, loose covers and curtains shaken and brushed, and the curtains pinned up out of the way. On this point Hannah Glasse advised, 'you should have little Rings to the bottom, three to each Curtain, fold them smooth, and hang the Rings on a Hook for the purpose'. Pictures, frames, stuccowork and ornaments were dusted by means of a pair of bellows. The housemaid is warned never to touch paintings with a brush

RULES to be Observed in this HALL.

1 WHOEVER is laft at Breakfaft to clear the Table, and put the Copper, Horns, Salt, Pepper &c, in their proper places, *or forfeit* ___ 3

2 THE fervants hall Cloth laid for Dinner by 1 oClock, and not omit laying the Salt, Pepper, and Spoons. ___ 3

3 THE houfe-keepers room Knives to be Clean'd ev'ry day by the Ufher of this hall. ___ 3

4 THAT if any Perfon be heard to Swear, or Ufe any Indecent language at any time when the Cloth is on the table. *He is to forfeit.* ___ 3

5 WHOEVER leaves any thing belonging to their Drefs or any Wearing Apparel out of their proper places. ___ 3

6 THAT no one be fuffered to Play at Cards in the Hall, before six oClock in the Evening. ___ 3

7 WHOEVER leaves any Pieces of Bread at Breakfaft, Dinner, or Supper. ___ 1

8 THAT if any one fhall be obferv'd cleaning livery clothes, or leather breeches, at any time of Meals; or fhall leave any dirt after cleaning them at any time. ___ 3

9 THAT the Ufher to have the Hall decently Swept, and the dirt taken away before dinner time. ___ 3

10 THAT no one fhall put any kind of provifions in any Cupboard or Drawer in the Hall after their meal but fhall return it from whence they had it. ___ 3

11 THAT the Table Cloth fhall after all meals be folded up, and put in the drawer for that purpofe. ___ 3

12 THAT if any one be obferv'd wipeing their Knives in the table cloth at any time. ___ 3

13 THAT if any ftable or other fervant take any plates to the ftable, or be feen to let them for Dogs to eat off ___ 3

14 THAT no wearing apparel to hang in the Hall, but fhall be put in the Clofets for that Purpofe. ___ 3

15 ALL ftable and other fervants to come to dinner with their Coats on. ___ 3

4. **An eighteenth-century set of rules, from the Servants' Hall at Clandon, Surrey.**

although she might, when necessary, wash them with a wet sponge and varnish them with egg-white![18]

In the eighteenth century, carpets were swept with a broom or whisk-broom and the furniture was then moved into the centre so that the carpet could be turned back all round and the floor swept with damp sand. Later authorities recommended sprinkling the carpet with wet tea-leaves. Whenever possible, carpets were turned over and walked on to loosen and expel dirt. The final task in the downstairs rooms was to polish the furniture with a waxed flannel and a soft cloth. The housemaid then turned her attention to the stairs, sweeping them with wet sand, dusting the handrail and tops

RULES *and* ORDERS, *to be* OBSERV'D *in this* HALL, *without* EXCEPTION.

1. Whoever is laft at Breakfaft, to clear the Table, and put the Copper, horns, Salt, Pepper, &c. in their proper places _____ or forfeit } 3

2. That the Poftilion, & Groom, fhall have the Servants hall cloth laid for Dinner, by one o'clock, and not omit laying Salt, Pepper, spoons, &c. _____ } 3

3. That the knives for Dinner, and the houfekeeper's room, to be clean'd ev'ry day, by the Poftilion, and Groom, and in cafe one if out the other do his bufinefs in his abfence, be it which it may _____ } 3

4. That if any Perfon, be heard to fwear, or ufe any indecent language, at any time when the Cloth is on the Table _____ } 3

5. Whoever leaves any powder, or pomatum, or any thing belonging to their drefs, or any wearing apparel, out of their proper places _____ } 3

6. That no one be fufferd to play at cards in this Hall, between fix in the Morning and fix in the Evening _____ } 3

7. Whoever leaves any pieces of Bread, at breakfaft, Dinner, or Supper 1

8. That if any one should be detected cleaning liverys, Cloaths, or leather Breeches, at any time of meals, or shall leave any dirt, after cleaning them, at any time _____ } 3

9. That the Poftilion, and Groom, to have the Hall, decently fwept, and the dirt taken away, before Dinner time _____ } 3

10. That every fervant, fhall afsift to pump Water for the ufe of the Houfe, every Wednefday _____ } 3

11. That no one fhall put any kind of Provifion in any Cupboard or Drawer, in the hall after their meals, but fhall return it from whence they had it _____ } 3

12. That the Table cloth, fhall after all meals, be folded up and put in the Drawer, for that purpofe _____ } 3

13. That if any one be detected wipeing their knives, in the Table cloth, at any time 3

14. That if any ftable, or other fervant, take any plates, to the ftable, or be feen to fet them for dogs, to eat off _____ } 6

15. That no wearing apparel, or hat boxes, be fufferd to hang in the Hall but fhall be put in the clofets, for that purpofe _____ } 3

Whoever defaces thefe RULES, in any manner _____ fhall forfeit 5/

5. Another set of servants' rules at Hatchlands, Surrey, probably by the same signwriter employed at Clandon.

6. **Madame Baccelli's footman and maid,** *c.* **1780. From a series of servants' portraits at Knole. (Collection Lord Sackville.)**

of doors and cleaning the cornice with a long-handled broom.

This might seem a full morning's work but, in fact, was done before the family rose. Where there was no lady's maid, the housemaid would also have to prepare the dressing-rooms. While the family was at breakfast, the maid could begin on the bed-rooms, opening shutters and windows, emptying and rinsing chamber-pots and then, with clean hands and apron, making the beds. Hangings were brushed with a clean soft brush and lifted onto the bed while the floor was swept with wet sand or a damp mop. The tops of canopied beds were protected from dust by paper tops which were changed twice yearly.

This daily general cleaning occupied the whole morning. The *Housekeeper's Oracle* suggested the following timetable for the housemaid:

Rise at Six,
Open Shutters by a quarter past,
Clean Grates by Seven,
Sweep Rooms by half past,
Dust and have Rooms ready by Eight,
Have your own Breakfast till half past,
Prepare all ready to go up Stairs by Nine,
Turn down Beds and open Windows by half past,
Clear away things, empty slops, and change water by Ten,
Make beds by Eleven,
Sweep Rooms by Twelve,
Dust and lay all smooth by one,
Clean yourself ready for Needlework, or whatever may be required, by half past.[19]

In addition to this daily routine, a more thorough

7. **The servants' hall at Chirk Castle, Clwyd, hung with eighteenth-century servants' portraits.**

cleaning usually took place once a week. This involved, in particular, scouring or dry-rubbing the floor-boards. Scouring had the disadvantage of leaving the room damp and most authorities advise that it should be done early in the morning and rarely, if at all, in winter. Stains were first removed with gall or, later, turpentine, and the boards were scrubbed with clean sand and cold water, always rubbing with the grain and drying the boards immediately with mops. Cold water was absorbed less quickly than hot and would not, therefore, darken the boards. Fuller's earth and, in the nineteenth and twentieth centuries, soda and carbolic soap were also used. Dry-rubbing entailed rubbing the boards with dry sand and then sweeping.

Advice on cleaning furniture was plentiful, but most polishes were based either on linseed oil, pure or coloured, or on beeswax and turpentine. Hannah Glasse advised using both:

As to Chair-frames, first rub them well with Linseed-oil, till you have got them quite clean, then with a dry cloth rub them bright; afterwards take a hard Brush and rub some yellow Wax on it, and brush the Frames well, and then with a woollen cloth rub them; thus they will keep the whole Year clean, every Day rubbing with that Flannel and a clean soft Duster.

Stains on furniture were removed by rubbing with finely powdered brick-dust, lemon-salts or a cork.

Most eighteenth-century housekeeping recipes sound quaint today since they relied on ingredients readily available in the house. Thus, paintwork was cleaned with stale beer and floorcloths with milk. Wallpaper was rubbed with stale bread, and tapestries and curtains were cleaned with bread, bran or potato pulp. A recipe for restoring the colour of black leather required the yolks of two newly-laid eggs and the white of one, gin and a

8. The Red (now White) Library at Petworth from a watercolour by Mrs. Percy Wyndham, *c.* 1860, showing loose 'case covers' on the chairs. (Collection Lord Egremont.)

9. The same room in 1926, showing how the use of loose covers continued into this century.

lump of sugar as well as blacking.[20]

Mirrors and gilt frames were among the most vulnerable furnishings and were sometimes left to the mistress of the house. Mirror glass was wiped with a damp cloth and polished with powdered chalk. The problem of cleaning carved frames was solved in the nineteenth century by covering them with gauze. Garlic and onion juice were believed to ward off flies and Mrs. Beeton's recipe 'To brighten Gilt Frames' involved boiling onions in water coloured with sulphur.

The housemaid's tools included a battery of brushes and brooms. Two bills of 1780 to Richard Colt Hoare at Stourhead, Wiltshire, list amongst other items, plate, furniture, dry-rubbing, whiteing, scrubbing and dusting brushes, and carpet, hearth, banister and long-hair brooms. A third bill, dated three years later, adds a long-scrubber, mops, picture brushes and whisks.[21] The contents of a housemaid's cupboard in 1915 had hardly changed; the only concession to modernity was a 'Patent carpet sweeper'.

In smaller households, the mistress often dabbled in housework. On one occasion, Jane Carlyle wrote to her husband that she had been 'helping Helen to scrub in the library till now – seven in the evening'.[22]

An important part of housekeeping involved protecting furnishings from dirt and damage. Loose covers were provided not only for chairs, but for almost every item in a room; commodes and tables had leather covers, carpets were covered with drugget and the bottoms of curtains were put into cotton 'bags'. Such covers were kept on for much of the time, even when the room was in normal use, and they protected the furnishings from wear and lessened the housemaid's work. They remained a familiar sight in country houses well into this century and, in recent years, their value has again been recognized and their use is being revived. The eighteenth century also understood the damage that sunlight could inflict on furniture, and housemaids were instructed to ensure that blinds were firmly closed when the sun was hot.

The running of a household depended on the observance of strict routine and the application of certain rules. In this way, family and guests could remain unaware of the activity going on around them; as one author noted:

'The work of the house is performed as if by magic, but it is the magic of system. . . . the whole goes on like well-oiled clockwork, where there is no noise nor jarring in its operations.'[23]

Notes

The methods and recipes quoted in the text are used purely to illustrate eighteenth-century practice. On no account should they be tried today without first obtaining expert advice.

[1] Samuel and Sarah Adams, *The Complete Servant*, London, 1825.

[2] Kent County Record Office, Maidstone: U269/E20/2 (by courtesy of Lord Sackville).

[3] West Sussex Record Office, Chichester: Petworth Papers, 570 (by courtesy of Lord Egremont).

[4] West Sussex Record Office: Petworth 627.

[5] West Sussex Record Office: Petworth 3112.

[6] Kent County Record Office: U1590/145 (Chevening, Kent; by courtesy of the Administrative Trustees of the Chevening Estate).

[7] 'The Household Book of Lady Grisell Baillie', in *Scottish History Society*, Series 2, vol. I, 1911.

[8] ed. Mary, Lady Verney, *Verney Letters of the 18th Century*, London, 1930, I, 1 Dec. 1710, p. 284; II, 8 Nov. 1741, p. 185.

[9] Kent County Record Office: U269/E80/3 and E. Stoddart Eckford and M. S. Fitzgerald, *Household Management*, London, 1915.

[10] Jane Welsh Carlyle to Jessie Hiddlestone, May 1865. (At Carlyle's House, 24 Cheyne Row, London SW3.)

[11] Kent County Record Office: U269/E17/6.

[12] West Sussex Record Office: Petworth 627.

[13] Gloucestershire County Record Office, Gloucester: D1799 E256.

[14] Jane W. Carlyle to Kate Sterling, Dec. 1851. (Carlyle's House.)

[15] Jane W. Carlyle to Jessie Hiddlestone, May 1865. (Carlyle's House.)

[16] Thea Holme, *The Carlyles at Home*, London, 1965.

[17] This résumé of housekeeping practice is compiled from: Hannah Glasse, *The Servants Directory and Housekeepers Companion*, London, 1760; *A New Present for a Servant Maid*, London, 1771; *The Young Woman's Companion*, Halifax, c. 1820; S. and S. Adams, *The Complete Servant*; Mrs. William Parkes, *Domestic Duties*, London, 1825 (2nd edition); *The Servants' Guide and Family Manual*, London, 1835 (4th edition); Mrs. Beeton, *Book of Household Management*, London, 1861. These works are to be found in the Brotherton Library, University of Leeds, which has a large collection of early cookery and housekeeping books.

[18] Hannah Glasse, op. cit.

[19] William Kitchiner, *The Housekeeper's Oracle*, London, 1829.

[20] *The Servant's Guide and Family Manual*, p. 131.

[21] Wiltshire County Record Office, Trowbridge: Stourhead Papers, 383/5: 81, 88, 170.

[22] Jane W. Carlyle to Thomas Carlyle, 25 Sept. 1845; in *Letters and Memorials of Jane Welsh Carlyle*, ed. J. A. Froude, London, 1883: vol. I, p. 346.

[23] Washington Irving, *Bracebridge Hall*, London, 1823 (first published 1822), p. 32.

Wicken Fen and the Swallowtail Butterfly

JOHN SMART

Wicken Fen is the oldest area in the United Kingdom designated and managed as a National Nature Reserve. It is now very accessible by car and the number of visitors recorded annually has reached about 40,000.

Back in the early nineteenth century the Fen was remarkably isolated and not much visited by naturalists. However, in 1851–52 Whittlesey Mere was finally drained and naturalists lost that paradise with its easy access from Peterborough. In 1860 Professor C. C. Babington in his *Flora of Cambridgeshire* wrote: 'There is scarcely a spot remaining (I know of one, near Wicken [village]) in which the ancient vegetation continues undisturbed and the land is sufficiently wet to allow of its coming to perfection.' Babington published a list of plants found at Wicken in his *Flora* and from that time forward naturalists, especially those associated with Cambridge, became interested in the Fen.

At this early stage of interest in the area, access was no easy matter. There was a ferry at Upware and also a congenial inn. Upware was reached by boat down the Cam, or perhaps on horse-back; the ferry was substantial and could have taken horses over the river to the inn. The inn at Upware was itself isolated and known as the 'Five Miles from Anywhere'.

Access to the Fen improved with the building of the railway from Cambridge to Ely with a station at Waterbeach. The big boost, however, came in 1884 with the final extension of the railway system to Mildenhall allowing access by Burwell or Soham, and many local people of Wicken became professionally interested in the naturalists' activities. The organization of an entomological visit by rail via Soham has been reconstructed vividly by Lt.-Col. A. M. Emmet (1972). The local experts were advised of impending arrival, and not only was transport from the station to Wicken and accommodation all laid on, but lamps were available for the nocturnal collecting of moths. The lamps were, of course, placed in favoured sites known to the professionals and one even suspects that if certain rarities were not on the wing on that particular night, specimens were liberated from match-boxes only to be triumphantly taken in the nets of the favoured visitors!

It was, however, the invention of the modern safety bicycle at the turn of the century that revolutionized visiting and research work on the Fen. An hour's vigorous pedalling over the hardly undulating roads through Waterbeach to Upware brought one to the ferry. A day's visit, independent of the professionals, now became easy from Cambridge. Movement around the Fen was also easier then than now because much of it was covered with sedge and litter fields and not with the scrub, or carr, of which there is so much today and which confines many visitors to the pathways, or slows them down if it is penetrated. Access by cycle and the ferry continued until around 1947, though by then the large ferry that could transport flocks of sheep and vehicles had been replaced by a row-boat that could still handle cycles. Use of the ferry had declined after the First World War because it was then that the concrete bridge was built over the Cam on the road between Wicken and Stretham. This bridge meant a longer route to the Fen from Cambridge but it allowed cars to get there easily. It also established entrance to the Fen at Wicken village as the norm, except for those who were frequent visitors and had one or more favoured entrances elsewhere.

Wicken Fen did not come into the possession of the National Trust as a unit. Individuals whose main interest appears to have been entomology, rather than botany or general natural history, had purchased parts of the area as they came on the market. Acquisition by the Trust through donation of parcels of land commenced in 1899 when J. C. Moberley presented an area of just over two acres (Gardiner, 1923). This was followed by other

1. **The Swallowtail Butterfly** (*Papilio machaon* **L.**).

2. **Swallowtail Butterfly, at rest showing the underside of the wings.**

3. **Wicken Lode looking west-south-west. The Sedge Fen is on the right; on the left of the Lode lies Adventurers'
Fen several feet below the water level in the Lode. The tower hide for watching birds on the Mere can be seen in
the middle distance.**

donations including one of about thirty acres given by N. C. Rothschild and a munificent gift of over 235 acres in 1911 by G. H. Verrall. Other gifts followed until the Wicken Fen property became as it stands today. There is no doubt whatsoever that the original donors in all cases presented land to the Trust in the interest of conserving a collecting ground for entomologists and particularly lepidopterists. Collecting and research has continued on the Fen but it has been controlled, at least since the 1930s, by the issue of permits. Gradually the issue of permits has had to be more and more carefully supervised because of the ever increasing numbers of visitors desiring permits, and it is more than likely that eventually collecting, other than for specified scientific investigations, may have to stop. This would bring Wicken into line with the arrangements on other National Trust properties of a like nature. The total area of Trust property now comprised in the Wicken Fen Nature Reserve is about 730 acres.

The property at Wicken is not enclosable by any means that would be financially possible at the present time. Enclosure would also change the nature of the Fen. There is a navigation, much used at the present time, from the Cam up the Wicken Lode to Wicken. This could be closed only by Act of Parliament. There are other rights of way onto, and within, the Fen that have some historical interest, in that their existence dates from the time when sedge, litter, reeds, sticks and peat were regularly cropped by owners of areas of the Fen or commoners who had an easement or right to take such crops. This cropping was governed by various customs all aimed at the maintenance of the productivity of the area. It was by no means a free-for-all. Fishing at the present time is poor.

At the time when the National Trust began acquisition the Fen was mainly covered by sedge and litter fields. This can be seen in photographs dating from that time and a little later. No doubt a few holdings had by neglect got bushed-up with

4. **Sedge Fen Drove looking east-north-east from Drainer's Dyke. This centuries-old drove served the local people for the removal of peat, sticks, sedge, reed and litter. These crops were also moved by boat on the Lode and on a network of connecting ditches many of which are now obsolete.**

carr, but the great areas of almost impenetrable carr now covering so much of the Fen, with the invasive birch trees, have developed since that time. One of the main objectives of recent management has been to recreate areas of sedge and litter fields, because these were the floristically interesting areas of the Fen. Carr has its interest, but it does not support the variety of other plants or other forms of life that the sedge and litter fields or the reed beds do. The taking of peat also produced conditions under which certain plants throve, growing on the recently exposed surfaces where the peat had been cut. While reeds and sedge can still be cropped and sold, a turbary on the scale that was carried out at Wicken would be totally uneconomic. All that can be done is to make small experimental exposures of peat periodically.

The glory of Wicken Fen was the swallowtail butterfly (*Papilio machaon* L.). This butterfly is also found in the Norfolk Broads, but the Wicken population was isolated and seems to have been slightly different from the Norfolk race. We have to speak of the Wicken swallowtails in the past tense. In spite of a strict limit set on the number of specimens that a collector could take (set out on the issued permit) the butterfly, having survived the 1939–45 War, died out at Wicken about 1950 (Smart, 1972). Collecting probably contributed to this, but it was certainly not the only factor.

The British swallowtail is a distinctive sub-species, *Papilio machaon britannicus* Seitz, of the species *Papilio machaon*. *Papilio machaon* comprises many other sub-species in Europe and eastwards, in isolated populations, as far as Japan, and a single sub-species in Alaska. Some of these sub-species are very closely related to each other but are distinguishable at sight by an expert. On the other hand, if specimens of the sub-species found in Japan were put side by side with British ones no one would hesitate to agree that they were distinctive. The swallowtail and all its sub-species were intensively studied, using biometrical methods, by

5. Sedge field. Cut sedge lies in front of standing sedge and carr can be seen beyond the standing sedge. Sedge and reed are both sold for thatching. Sedge is cut in the summer, reed in winter.

Dr. Karl Eller (1936). When specimens from all the sub-species are examined they can be arranged in such a way as to show the phylogenetic relationships of the sub-species to each other, and this suggests the way in which they have descended from a common, unknown and now extinct, ancestor.

The swallowtail butterfly is a species that, like many others, owes its present-day pattern of sub-species and their distribution to forced migration consequent on gradual changes in climate and vegetation during the more recent Ice Ages. These changes isolated populations of the butterfly in various places, and this isolation led to the development of distinctive features which enabled Eller to work out his scheme of classification into sub-species. He elaborated his views in a paper published in 1939.

The history of the swallowtail in England has been reviewed by Bretherton (1951), and anyone interested should also consult Warren's paper

(1949) dealing with matters of sub-specific nomenclature. At one time the butterfly was widely distributed from the Midlands and East Anglia southwards. Relatively few specimens with authentic recorded data survive from the years preceding the middle of the nineteenth century and Bretherton's review is largely based on a critical consideration of published plates along with published records. It would seem probable that the true British swallowtail (sub-species *britannicus*) at one time reached as far south as the Thames and was to be found around the estuary and up the valley of the river for some distance. Old records from the southern counties were probably all of the sub-species *bigeneratus* Verity which is found in Continental Europe along the Channel coast. There is every indication that in the late eighteenth and early nineteenth centuries there were breeding populations of *bigeneratus* in Kent, Sussex and elsewhere. These should, perhaps, be called colonies of the European form; they may have persisted for a few years and then died out. There may have been differences between the climate of today and that of 150 – 200 years ago which favoured the existence of these colonies. However, the extension of ever more intensive methods of agriculture must have had their effect on the butterfly, mainly because of the extensive and efficient drainage works that were put in hand at that time and earlier.

It thus came about that the British swallowtail was confined to the Cambridge Fens and the Norfolk Broads by the middle of the nineteenth century and that by the beginning of the twentieth century the Broads population was probably completely isolated from the relict Cambridge Fenland population at Wicken. It is interesting to note that Dempster, King and Lakhani (1976) have reported that they believe there are small morphological differences between specimens from the Norfolk Broads and specimens from the Wicken population preserved in collections.

One of the peculiarities of the British swallowtail is that its caterpillars are highly selective about their food plant. This is *Peucedanum palustre*, commonly called milk parsley, or, at Wicken, 'the Carrot'. They can be fed on *Angelica* but do not seem to select this plant as food naturally. The growth of large areas of carr and the reduction of areas of sedge and litter, coupled with some other factors, have led to a great decrease in the quantity and quality of milk parsley available for the butterflies to lay their eggs on. In this respect the British swallowtail differs from its cousins in Europe and elsewhere, which are much more catholic in their selection of larval food plant. In fact, some of these immigrating cousins come over from the Continent and are known to lay their eggs on the foliage of culinary carrots, but they do not seem able to establish themselves permanently; these immigrating butterflies do not reach Wicken. Further details about the British swallowtail will be found in such classic texts as Barrett (1899) or

6. **Stack of reed, and punt, at the Staithe. Wicken village is slightly elevated above the level of the Sedge Fen and the Lode. Lode Lane leads from Wicken village to the Staithe, the head of the navigation which extends down the Lode to the river Cam at Upware and thence to the sea at King's Lynn.**

7. **Fully grown larva of the Swallowtail Butterfly on flowering Milk Parsley** (*Peucedanum palustre* (**L**) **Moench**).

in more recent books such as Howarth (1973).

When the swallowtail disappeared from Wicken in 1950 (Smart, 1972), a number of attempts were made to re-introduce it from Norfolk. None of these attempts was successful. More recently, however, another attempt has been made by Dr. J. P. Dempster of Monks Wood Experimental Station. Larger numbers of butterflies were reared for liberation than in previous attempts and about 2,000 seedlings of the caterpillar's food plant were planted out in various parts of the Trust's property. Added to this, the extensive clearance of carr has created a far larger area of suitable habitat for the butterfly than was present in the early 1950s. The details of this introduction have been published in *Nature in Cambridgeshire* (Dempster, 1976). What can

be reported is that many butterflies were seen on the Fen in 1976 which must have been the progeny of those liberated in 1975. The numbers were sufficient to make those responsible feel that an effective re-introduction had been made. However, the abnormal drought during the summer of 1976 has led to a drastic reduction in the butterfly's numbers, and fewer can be expected on the Fen in 1977. It remains to be seen whether the butterfly persists at Wicken, but there appears to be a good chance if it survives the exceptionally unfavourable drought conditions of 1976. For the time being, collecting of the swallowtail will not be allowed at Wicken and would, in any case, be pointless as all of the butterflies seen will be descendants of the laboratory-reared stock liberated in 1975.

Bibliography

C. C. Babington, *Flora of Cambridgeshire*, (London, 1860).

C. G. Barrett, *The Lepidoptera of the British Isles*, **1**: pp. 13–16, (London, 1899).

R. F. Bretherton, 'The early history of the swallow-tail butterfly (*Papilio machaon* L.) in England', *Entomologist's Rec. J. Var.*, **63**: pp. 206–211. (1951).

J. P. Dempster, 'The Swallowtail Butterfly at Wicken Fen', *Nature in Cambridgeshire*, No. **19**: pp. 11–14. (1976).

J. P. Dempster, M. L. King and K. H. Lakhani, 'The status of the Swallowtail Butterfly in Britain', *Ecological Entomology*, **1**: pp. 71–84. (1976).

K. Eller, 'Die Rassen von *Papilio machaon* L.', *Abh. Bayer. Akad. Wiss.*, *N.F.*, **36**: pp. 1–96. (1936).

K. Eller, 'Fragen und Probleme zur Zoogeographie und zur

Rassen- und Artbildung in der *Papilio machaon*-Gruppe', *Verh. 7 internat. Kongr. Ent.*, **1**: pp. 74–101. (1939).

A. M. Emmet, Presidential Address, *Proc. Brit. Ent. Nat. Hist. Soc.*, **5** (2): pp. 46–74. (1972).

J. S. Gardiner, *Natural History of Wicken Fen*, (Cambridge, 1923–32).

T. G. Howarth, *South's British Butterflies* (London, 1973).

J. Smart, 'Butterflies and day-flying moths', *Guides to Wicken Fen*, No. **8**: pp. 1–13, National Trust: Wicken Fen Local Committee. (1972).

B. C. S. Warren, 'A note on the Central European races of *Papilio machaon* and their nomenclature', *Entomologist*, **82**: pp. 150–153. (1949).

Staying at Felbrigg as the Guest of Wyndham Ketton-Cremer

BRINSLEY FORD

If I had to rely solely on my memory I could only recall in rather general terms what life at Felbrigg was like as the guest of Wyndham Ketton-Cremer. I know that what struck me most about staying there was the quiet and ordered way of life, which stemmed from my host's calm and equable temperament, and this in turn was rooted in his firm Christian beliefs and practices. I have never stayed in any other house where there was such an atmosphere of peace and serenity, so much so that it must be admitted that some of Wyndham's more lively friends found life at Felbrigg too becalmed and monastic.

Fortunately, I do not have to depend on my memory, for in those days I kept a journal in which I have recorded short accounts of my seven visits to Felbrigg. These accounts were based on jottings made while everything, and particularly Wyndham's conversation, was still fresh in my mind, for I have always taken to heart the observation made by my great-grandfather, Richard Ford, that 'a note made on the spot is worth a cart-load of recollections'.

My wife and I paid our first visit to Felbrigg in May 1953. 'The spring is always cold and late on the Norfolk coast' is the opening sentence in Wyndham's great book, FELBRIGG: THE STORY OF A HOUSE (1962), and he goes on to say: 'For weeks at a time the wind blows in from the sea, a chill drying wind, northerly or easterly'. In May 1953, the weather was no exception. I think it was generally agreed that Felbrigg was one of the coldest houses in England. There is nothing but a belt of trees to protect it from the icy Arctic winds that sweep in from the North Sea. I remember that one of Wyndham's most distinguished American friends, who shared his interest in Horace Walpole, told me that he found the cold at Felbrigg so unendurable that he went in to Cromer on some trumped-up excuse to buy himself the thickest set of long woollen combinations he could find.

Although our visit took place in May it was still far too cold to inhabit the grand suite of rooms in the West wing, so we lived and had all our meals in the Great Hall (Fig. 3). This was heated fairly effectively by a large and ugly anthracite stove round which we sat on the few chairs that were not piled high with books waiting to be reviewed.

To make up for the cold, everything was done to make us as comfortable as possible, and our bedrooms were warmed by oil stoves. There was no electricity in the house so we read by lamps and went to bed by candles and enjoyed the pleasant illusion of living in the past. The house was run on old-fashioned lines by a staff of three. This consisted of Ward, the butler, who had already been at Felbrigg for thirty years, a maid and a cook. At this date the reign of Mrs. Muffin in the kitchen had not yet begun, but subsequent guests will remember being taken by Wyndham at the end of a visit to see Mrs. Muffin and to admire the rows of highly-polished copper pots and pans arrayed on the dressers. On these occasions Wyndham would always make a point of looking out of the window so as to give his guests an opportunity of endorsing their compliments to Mrs. Muffin with something more precious than copper.

I have never much cared for the baser metals, but the brass can filled with hot water, which Ward produced in the morning and again in the evening when one went up to dress for dinner, was always a welcome sight. It was placed in the blue willow-patterned basin and wrapped in a towel to keep the water hot. The day started with early morning tea, when Ward removed one's clothes, bringing them back with the London dust brushed out of them, and one's shoes sparklingly polished. The meals were at the same appointed hours as in other houses, but the guests were expected to be punctual.

On one of my visits Wyndham had invited an old friend of his and of mine to stay. This friend had been a boyhood contemporary of Wyndham's at

1. Wyndham Ketton-Cremer, by Allan Gwynne-Jones, R.A. Painted in 1969, in the dining room at Felbrigg.

2. **Felbrigg Hall from the south-west, showing the Jacobean entrance front with William Samwell's wing, completed in 1687, on the left.**

Harrow. They were fond of each other, but they led very different lives, the friend being about as wilful, capricious and moody as Wyndham was steady and dependable. At five minutes to eight on the evening of our arrival, I looked in on our friend on my way down to dinner. I found him reclining like a pasha in a dressing-gown on a window-seat enjoying the lovely view and the balmy summer evening and listening to a reading of modern poetry on his own portable wireless-set. Through the haze of his cigar smoke I caught sight of a half-empty bottle of gin. When the gong sounded I hurried downstairs, two steps at a time, to find Wyndham waiting impatiently in the Great Hall. As Ward handed me a small glass of sherry on a silver tray, I noticed that my host was fidgeting with his watch. As the minutes went by and his other guest failed to appear, Wyndham's expression can best be likened to the calm surface of a lake being gradually ruffled by an approaching storm. Finally, after waiting with increasing tension for twenty-five minutes the storm burst, Wyndham rushed from the room and thunder was heard at the top of the stairs. I caught the sound of our friend's

voice pleading for another five minutes grace, and Wyndham's incensed reply that his establishment could not be kept waiting a moment longer. This was the only occasion on which I saw Wyndham really angry. At dinner our friend exerted his great charm, and this combined with our host's natural good humour caused the incident to be quickly forgotten.

Except on our first and freezing visit, the meals always took place in the beautiful dining-room designed by James Paine. Nothing could be happier than the effect of the white rococo plaster-work against the lilac-coloured walls. The plaster-work was executed by Joseph Rose, one of the masters of his craft, and the elegant stucco frames, with their swags of fruit and flowers, were made to set off the fine family portraits by Lely. The food was not as imaginative as the decoration. But it was English food at its best. And who could want anything better than lobsters from Sheringham, lamb cutlets with broad beans or peas or asparagus freshly picked from the garden, followed by gooseberry or red-currant pie with cream from the farm. The cellar was well-stocked with fine clarets and port, and given Wyndham's abstemious habits there was never any chance of its running dry.

By the time we paid our second visit to Felbrigg in July 1958, electric light had been installed, but otherwise everything seemed unchanged and life there continued on its placid course. I noted in my journal after this visit that the Orangery, which dates from about 1705, was being re-roofed as it had fallen into a bad state of repair.

I have always imagined that Wyndham was very well off, but he lived simply, yet comfortably and without any ostentation. All the money he could spare was spent on the house, the outbuildings, and the estate. He was a wonderful landlord. I remember his saying to me rather wistfully, when we were looking at a picture, how much he would have liked

to have had it cleaned, but he hesitated to do so, knowing that for the money it would cost him he might be able to make some improvements to his tenants' cottages which could make all the difference to the comfort of their lives.

Wyndham took great pleasure in showing the pictures and books at Felbrigg to anyone capable of appreciating them. It was a memorable experience to stand in the dingy light of the Gothic library, for the blinds were always kept drawn to protect the bindings, while Wyndham pulled some venerable tomes from their shelves and expatiated on their contents. There was one volume that had belonged to Dr. Johnson, and Wyndham liked to attribute its battered condition to the fact that it had been much handled by the sage he so much admired, and with whom he had so many virtues in common.

3. **The Great Hall at Felbrigg.**

4. The Dining Room, designed by James Paine in 1750.

The room that enchanted me most at Felbrigg was the Cabinet. This was the room which William Windham had planned to display the pictures collected on his Grand Tour from which he returned in 1742. This room (Fig. 6) gives the impression of having remained intact since William Windham's day, and its most notable feature is the series of charming gouache views of Rome and its environs by Giovanni Battista Busiri.

A tour of the garden with Wyndham was no less instructive and delightful than a tour of the house. I have recorded in my journal my recollections of a stroll with him one summer afternoon when he led the way to the kitchen-garden swinging a long instrument for cutting weeds. His comments about everything that caught his eye were as well-informed as those of a learned member of the Horticultural Society, but they were enriched by

metaphor. Here is a sample that I scribbled down the same evening.

> Those Thuya trees are some of the oldest in England and their stems resemble some of Barbara Hepworth's dendrological shapes. The pheasants love those trees for roosting and the keepers also love them as the pheasants cannot be detected by the poachers in all that fuzz. On other trees the pheasants present a sitting target, and the poachers have an uncanny skill for bringing them down with ball-bearings fired from a catapult. The wood of the trees is very valuable, and even the leaves can be sold as floral tributes.

In the kitchen-garden Wyndham took us into the glass-houses where there were some exotic plants. 'I always have a few ginger plants', he remarked, 'as I like to have their musky scent wafting through the house'. Perhaps, in his

5. **The Drawing Room.**

memory, the National Trust might make a point of always having some of these plants at Felbrigg.

In the centre of the kitchen-garden stands the Dovehouse. Wyndham records in his book that it had fallen into a ruinous state 'with gaping holes in the roof, the principal timbers rotted through, and the cupola leaning drunkenly awry'. It was reconstructed by him in 1937. Wyndham took us into the Dovehouse, which has niches for 2,000 birds, and this led him to give us a vivid account of the food problems confronting a household in the eighteenth century; he cited the fact that only 'Seigneurs' had the right to keep columbariums in France as one of the causes of the French Revolution.

Far more than the garden Wyndham loved his woods, which were his 'joy and pride'. For, like his books, they were essentially his creation, and he loved his trees down to their roots, and to the roots

of his being. Each tree was a friend, and he watched over it with a solicitude which few people bestow upon their friends. Wyndham knew a great deal about forestry and was very shocked at the way the estate had been neglected by his great-uncle, whom, in his book, he accused of not having planted a single tree between 1900 and his death in 1935. Wyndham set out to remedy this regrettable situation and during his tenure of Felbrigg he planted a vast number of trees. I once asked him how many; he answered in his conservative way that, while his agent estimated the number at 250,000, he would not care to name the figure beyond saying that it certainly exceeded 100,000.

It was, perhaps, on a perambulation of his woods with Wyndham that one became most aware of the duality of his nature, for he combined some of the characteristics of the Norfolk squire with those of a Virgilian poet. But in dealing with matters on his estate the former role was uppermost for, much as he loved a Claudian vista, I do not think that he would have felt justified in creating one if it meant sacrificing a number of valuable trees.

In my journal I have recorded how he took me on an unforgettable tour of his woods when I was staying with him in September 1963. As I hardly know one tree from another, my ignorance must have been as trying to Wyndham as it would be to me if I had to take someone round a picture gallery who did not know the difference between a Renoir and a Rembrandt. But Wyndham was wonderfully patient, and I suspect that he quite enjoyed showing me what were, after all, the results of one of the creative sides of his life of which he was most proud. We drove to the woods in his car and were soon strolling in the spacious halls made by the beech trees on carpets of leaves as soft underfoot and as richly tinted as rugs from Shiraz or Isfahan. When we emerged from the cool shadows of the beeches, we came to grass walks between plantations of young trees. Wyndham pointed out to me that he always planted cherry trees along the edges of some of his plantations, for the sheer delight of their blossom in the spring, and that in the middle of them he planted a mountain ash, so that its red berries should provide a splash of colour in the autumn. This was a touch worthy of Turner, whose scarlet buoys relieve the monotony of his green tempestuous seas.

On our walk Wyndham knocked the head off a harmless looking mushroom. It had a grey speckled top and was white underneath.

> That, he observed, is the death-head variety, and those who eat it die the most painful death. It is the subject of one of Agatha Christie's thrillers. It is far more lethal than the one which has red spots, like danger signals, and which looks so very much more poisonous, but which gives one a not altogether unpleasant form of delirium from which one gradually recovers.

The climax of our walk was a viewpoint on which there had formerly stood a majestic oak. This viewpoint (Fig. 7) was at the foot of a V, and commanded two vast avenues, in size worthy of Blenheim or Versailles, which had been planted by Wyndham to commemorate VE Day. Alas! the oak, which had been intended as the focal point of both avenues, had been struck by lightning and all that remained of it was a tell-tale stump. 'In my old age', Wyndham observed, 'when I am crippled by gout, I had looked forward to being dragged up here by a pony-cart or its modern equivalent and, sitting under the shade of the oak, being able to admire the avenues I had planted, but, as you see, this hope has been thwarted'. I pleaded that he should erect an obelisk on the spot where the oak had stood. He said that he would have approved of this in a more leisurely age but he did not now wish to be 'bracketed with a Lord Berners'. His modest plan for the viewpoint was to have a semi-circular bench on a platform. The photograph shows (Fig. 7) what has been done. It was a hot day and there was a haze on the horizon of both vistas. At the end of the right-hand vista, Wyndham explained, one could ordinarily see the tower (or was it the spire?) of the church at Sall, while at the end of the vista on the left he had hoped that one would be able to see the spire of Norwich Cathedral, but, as this was not possible, all that could be seen on a clear day was the top of 'Crome's beloved Mousehold Heath'.

On our way back to Felbrigg, Wyndham showed me the 'Oval' wood mentioned in his book. This had been excluded from any concessions allowed to him by the Forestry Commission. Now, he told me, he got on very well with this body, but, shortly after the war, he had had difficulties with its representatives who were 'left-wing young men who thought of nothing except planting parallelograms of twenty acres of spruce which they are no doubt now doing in Africa where most of them have gone'.

Wyndham kept a constant eye on his plantations, noting the growth of the trees, and I remember on another occasion his pointing to a small plantation of firs and regretting that they had been 'decimated by the frost-laden wind'. Now that I have tried to give some idea of Wyndham's love of his woods, I think one could pay no greater tribute to his generosity than to mention the fact that every summer he allowed an East End troop of scouts to camp among his finest woods, incurring the risk of fire and of the boys being tempted to carve their initials, or worse, on the bark of his beloved trees.

I have written in my journal that as I walked behind Wyndham on that September afternoon 'his portly figure made even more shapeless by an old macintosh, his grey hair straggling onto his collar beneath a green pork-pie hat, his slightly gouty step supported by a walking-stick, I was not unaware that I was treading in the wake of one who already ranks as one of Norfolk's worthies, and whose memory will be treasured in years to come'.

6. The Cabinet, hung with pictures acquired by William Wyndham II on his Grand Tour between 1738 and 1742.

Although Wyndham looked rather robust, he was really very delicate, his health having been injured at an early age by attacks of rheumatic fever. In spite of this he led a very strenuous life, managing to find time for his writing while undertaking countless public duties. To someone of his temperament the most exacting of these duties was his term (1951–52) as High Sheriff of Norfolk. In describing his experiences to me he said that for someone 'so shy and withdrawn' as himself (these were his very words), it had been something of an ordeal. Worst of all, he had been called upon, as part of his duties, to witness two hangings, and painful though this must have been to him, he felt that he was performing a duty which was no more frightful than that which many soldiers had to face in the last war. He was always haunted by the death of his brother, Dick, who had died of wounds, perhaps 'in agony and loneliness', during the German invasion of Crete in 1941.

During his long service as a J.P. – he became a magistrate in 1934 and was Chairman of the Cromer Bench from 1948 to 1966 – Wyndham learnt much about the seamy side of life in Norfolk. He used to tell me about some of the strange cases that were brought before him. Perhaps the oddest was that of the man whose strange perverted sexual mania took the harmless though trying form of what Wyndham described as 'raping ladies' bicycles'. Before the man's arrest many an elderly spinster or carefree schoolgirl had been informed by the police that their bicycles had been found rudely assaulted and buckled in a ditch. These stories lost nothing through being told in the same rounded periods and well-turned phrases in which he might have narrated some stirring episode in the Civil War in Norfolk.

Wyndham, as he was only too ready to admit, was a shy man, and this was reflected in his conversation by the fact that he seldom looked anyone straight in the face; the glance from his large brown eyes always seemed to be sliding away from one. But there was nothing shy about his delivery, which flowed as smoothly as the Danube. He chose his words with the same care that he did in his writings. He was an enemy of exaggeration. He told me that when he first heard his voice recorded for a broadcast, he could not believe that the 'rich fruity accents' were his own. It was certainly a voice that gave one the impression of having been nurtured on vintage port rather than on dry martinis. His conversation never palled for he was never assertive or repetitive, and at every turn of

his discourse one became more and more aware of how widely read and richly informed he was on every conceivable subject. In the course of the evening he might discover that one was interested in the collections formed by Sir Andrew Fountaine at Narford, that one had never read the account of the visit to Norfolk in the eighteenth-century by a young member of the La Rochefoucauld family, that one had never even heard of Kilvert's Diary, with the result that on retiring for the night one was given the relevant books to satisfy one's curiosity, only to find by one's bed various books which he thought one might enjoy – Dorothy Stroud's *Humphry Repton* (probably to prepare one for a visit to H. T. S. Upcher at Sheringham Park), Mary Woodhall's edition of Gainsborough's Letters, and Cyril Connolly's book on French Pavilions.

Wyndham delighted in anecdote, especially when it concerned his neighbours in Norfolk. Great was his amusement on hearing that when some learned Norwich Society had visited one of the great houses in Norfolk, the noble owner had welcomed the party with the remark that he always enjoyed showing his house to 'artisans'. Not unnaturally this remark had given great offence, which was not intended, for, as Wyndham explained, the nobleman's vocabulary was both limited and uncertain, and the word that this Lord Malaprop had mistakenly used was evidently mixed up in his mind with that for art-lovers.

Wyndham was never malicious and gently repressed those who made catty remarks in his presence. He could not bear it when people said unkind things about his friends, and when some visitor was guilty of this crime and was foolish enough to ignore Wyndham's warning signals to be silent, he got a sharp rebuke, for, on such occasions, in his quiet way, Wyndham could be very formidable. Of course there were a few people who, for just reasons, had incurred his wrath, and on their failings it would have required a saint-like abnegation to remain mute. Outraged by the behaviour of a selfish woman towards her son and daughter-in-law, who were friends of his, Wyndham remarked to me that the old lady was 'pickled in a sauce of disagreeability'.

On every visit to Felbrigg, Wyndham provided some delightful expedition to look forward to. He would take one to luncheon with Thelma de Chair at Blickling, to the Bacons at Raveningham, or to the Blofelds at Hoveton. Driving sedately at the wheel of his rather old-fashioned car, Wyndham would expatiate in his mellifluous tones on a

7. The avenues at Felbrigg planted by Wyndham Ketton-Cremer to commemorate V.E. Day, 1945.

chosen theme. On one of our last drives together, he got on to the subject of the dangers of interfering with nature by introducing alien species into this country. After describing the menace of nutria, which he said had done untold damage when they had escaped from their farms round the Suffolk Broads, he went on to tell me how the name of Lord Lilford, a distinguished ornithologist, was cursed for having brought into this country some little owls from Spain which, unlike our English owls, were a great pest. I forget why the species of dormouse introduced by one of the Rothschilds became so unpopular, but it was characteristic of Wyndham's conversation to recall that it was the same kind of dormouse that was considered such a delicacy by the Romans who 'eat it stewed in honey and sprinkled with poppy seeds as mentioned by Petronius in his account of Trimalchio's feast'.

During one's stay at Felbrigg, Wyndham always made a point of inviting to a meal people whom he knew that one would like to meet. Remembering my rather morbid interest in the Russian Revolu-

tion he invited to luncheon Sir Thomas and Lady Preston. Sir Thomas had married his charming Russian wife in Ekaterinburg in 1913, and he was British Consul in that town when the Tsar and his family were murdered there in 1918. Sir Thomas subsequently gave me his book *Before the Curtain* (1950) in which he describes the terrible events which took place in the basement of the house of Epatieff. At the luncheon Sir Thomas revealed that he was eighty-three, and busily engaged in writing an operetta about the Congress of Vienna. This luncheon took place on our last visit to Felbrigg in July, 1969. By then Wyndham was snugly established in what he called his 'retreat'. This Lilliputian abode Wyndham had created for himself in the north-west corner of the courtyard. His small dining-room, he told me, had in former times been a game-larder, a dairy, and a laundry. Everything was given up to comfort at the expense of beauty and elegance. A few unexciting modern pictures hung on the walls of his sitting-room, which contained two radiators in addition to an electric

8. The brasses of Simon and Roger de Felbrigg and their wives.

fire. There was also a television set and a radio-gram. Upstairs the bedrooms, with their Morris chintz curtains, were small and comfortable with bathrooms and loos close at hand in the corridor. But it must be frankly admitted that this annexe to the main house, in which I am glad to say we spent a lot of time and had tea in the afternoon, had little to distinguish it, except its minuteness and comfort, from the annexe of any modern provincial hotel.

No account of staying with Wyndham at Felbrigg would be complete without some mention of his love for the small medieval church which stands isolated in the park. When his parents inherited Felbrigg the church had fallen into a 'condition of the most shocking neglect'. They put it in order, and their son cherished it. Wyndham was a deeply religious man. Sunday after Sunday he sat in his pew, and knelt to receive the sacrament of Holy Communion at the altar. When he showed us the church on our first visit, he took flowers for his parents' graves. Everything he did for the church was partly an act of filial piety. For instance, he installed electric lighting and heating in the church in memory of his mother. He preserved and guarded the monuments zealously, and I remember noting how carefully he had protected the wonderful early fifteenth-century brasses of Sir Simon and Lady Felbrigg with two layers of drugget. In my journal I find that I have recorded the visit to the church of some learned Society, when Wyndham, at the invitation of the vicar, mounted the pulpit and gave a fascinating talk about the history of the church and its monu-ments. Pointing to the fine bust of William Wind-ham by Nollekens, he regretted that it 'had been built into the sedilia with that disregard which unfortunately the eighteenth-century manifested towards everything medieval'. After visiting the church, Wyndham drove an old lady, aged eighty-three, whom he described as 'sweet but ignorant', back across the park to tea at Felbrigg, while we followed, like a funeral procession, on foot with the rooks laughing at us overhead. Another, sadder cortège followed Wyndham's ashes to the church on 17 December 1969. Seven years earlier he had ended the Prelude to his book on Felbrigg with the words:

> I have tried to hold the house and estate together during my own span of life. And I hope that in the course of time my ashes will lie in the churchyard among the plover-haunted fields.

Note

Portrait of Wyndham Ketton-Cremer, Painted in 1969 *by Allan Gwynne-Jones, R.A.* (Fig. 1).
As a footnote to these recollections of staying at Felbrigg, I must put on record a few facts about the portrait at Felbrigg of Wyndham by Allan Gwynne-Jones, since I was responsible for persuading him to commission it. Knowing that Wynd-ham admired the portrait of Sir Edmund Bacon and other works by Gwynne-Jones, I first proposed that he should also sit for him in 1967. Wyndham was sympathetic to the idea but he was then committed to the expense of creating his new quarters in the north-west corner of the courtyard and decided that the matter must be set aside for the time being. Then, if I remember correctly, he had to spend a lot of money on the roof at Felbrigg. At all events, it was not until March, 1969, that he wrote to tell me that he had taken the plunge, and had asked Gwynne-Jones to paint the portrait. The Visitors'

Book at Felbrigg shows that Gwynne-Jones stayed there from July 14–22, August 4–9, September 8–19. A further visit was planned but, for some reason, did not take place, and when Wyndham died, aged 63, on 12 December 1969, the portrait was still unfinished. At my suggestion the artist afterwards did as little to the painting as possible for fear of losing its immediacy.

The portrait was painted in the Paine dining-room at Felbrigg, partly because Wyndham was very fond of this room, partly because of the light which was much better than in the older part of the house. Wyndham's friends differ in their reactions to this portrait, but to me it seems to have captured, far better than the camera ever did, something of that modesty and gentleness that lightened the heavy Gibbonian features of the squire and the scholar, who was one of the most distinguished writers of our day.

Rise and Demise of a Wren Church:
the Reredos from St. Matthew Friday Street at Polesden Lacey

JOHN KENWORTHY-BROWNE

The strangest feature at Polesden Lacey is, without much doubt, the great oak carving against the fireplace wall in the hall (Fig. 1). On a casual glance it might well appear typical of the 'Queen Anne Revival' at full flood. However, the excellent quality of the carving is obvious on a closer look, and the cherub's head and panels below recall, incongruously enough, the City churches of London. The visitor will be informed that this is, in fact, the altar-piece or reredos from a Wren church, St. Matthew Friday Street, and was carved by Edward Pearce.

The church of St. Matthew stood on the west side of Friday Street in Faringdon Ward Within, just south of Cheapside and close to the site of the former St. Paul's Cross (Fig. 2). How long a church had been there is not known, but it seems first to be recorded in the *Taxatio* of Pope Nicholas IV in 1291 as 'S. Matheus in Fridaystret'. The parish was vested in the Abbey of Westminster. After the Suppression the patron was the Bishop of Westminster, and then, under Edward VI, the Bishop of London. Friday Street, Stow tells us, was 'so called of the fishmongers dwelling there and serving Friday's market', though the fish sellers were probably more active in the southern part of the street where it met with Old Fish Street.

After the Great Fire of 1666, St. Matthew's was rebuilt, and united with the former and rather larger neighbouring parish of St. Peter West Cheap (Fig. 3). St. Peter's had been at the corner of Cheapside and Wood Street, and it survives still as a tiny open space behind iron railings. Here a famous plane tree looks over a little row of old two-room houses, whose lessees apparently were always forbidden to build higher. In 1797, Wordsworth wrote a lyric inspired by a thrush singing here, and as late as 1850 two rooks nested in the branches. Churches in this neighbourhood were formerly numerous, and since 1666 St. Vedast Foster Lane has come to cover no fewer than

thirteen parishes, including those of St. Matthew and St. Peter. Some of the demolished churches are recorded by plaques. But no visible record remains now of St. Matthew's, and the north section of Friday Street has disappeared into Victor Heal's new Bank of England extension.

The church of the United Parishes of St. Matthew Friday Street and St. Peter West Cheap, serving 117 houses, was begun in 1682, and opened on 29 November, 1685, nineteen years after the fire. In the meantime, the parishioners had been served by a wooden 'tabernacle', erected in 1673 and costing £168.12s.12d. The rebuilding of St. Matthew's, the cheapest and plainest of all Wren's City churches, cost £2,381.8s.2d. The ground was 'small and inconveniently sited'. To the east, Friday Street was narrow; the other three sides were overshadowed by tall houses. The fenestration was peculiar, and the central part of the church was not well lit. In 1738, the surveyor had to advise against opening up a new window near the pulpit because it would give only a dim 'Reflective Light'.

The back walls and the plain tower (containing a bell cast in 1704) were of brick with stone dressings. But the east end standing over Friday Street was of Portland stone, and its elevation was distinctive. In 1883, when its destruction was imminent, A. H. Mackmurdo wrote of the 'splendid range of five repeated windows, with their carved archivolts, sculptured caps and cherubic keystones . . . having an elegance rare in all these churches, and withal crowned by a cornice of very individual design' (Figs. 5 and 6). No drawing by Wren for this church survives, and it has been assumed that he did little more than provide a sketch. But as yet no evidence has been found to indicate what the mason, Edward Pearce, may have contributed to the design. The only contract discovered among the building records in St. Paul's Cathedral Library is dated 18 May 1683, for the carpenter, John Longland, 'to make & erect a hipped roofe . . .

1. **Polesden Lacey, Surrey. View of the Hall, showing the Reredos from St. Matthew Friday Street.**

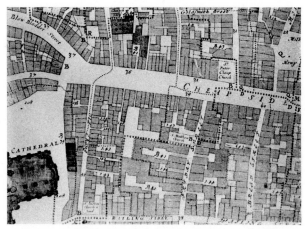

2. **London before the Fire. Detail from Faithorne's Map (1658), showing: St. Matthew Friday Street (no. 71), St. Peter West Cheap (no. 90), and St. Vedast Foster Lane (no. 32).**

3. **London after the Fire. Detail from Ogilby's Map (1676), showing the site of St. Matthew's in Friday Street (not yet rebuilt) and St. Peter's Churchyard.**

attending to ye orders & direction of Sr Chr. Wren . . .' All the various contractors, including the mason, were paid directly from Wren's office, and there is no reference as to how the mason co-operated with the bricklayer or carpenter.

The inside dimensions, though not quite regular, were roughly a double cube, nearly 60 feet long, 33 feet wide and 31 feet high. The plastering was simple, but the lantern effect of the east end was dramatic (Fig. 8). In 1839, George Godwin, who disliked Wren's churches, wrote that St. Matthew's 'certainly has no ecclesiastical character', though he allowed that 'the Altar-piece at the east end displays some good specimens of carving [and] the

pulpit is a good piece of workmanship'. The wainscotting of oak, grained, was ten feet high, and the square or 'double' box pews rose to 5 ft. 10 in. During the nineteenth century this proved too difficult, and in 1862 the last Rector, Rev. W. Sparrow Simpson, reluctantly had the church reseated and the height of the pews reduced. At the west end there was a huge window overlooking the gallery, and the font was below. A small organ was installed by 1738, but George England made a better one in 1762 with three manuals and sixteen stops. Pedals were added in 1790, and this organ was doubled in size in 1862.

The furnishings, pews and wainscotting were

4. **St. Matthew Friday Street. Engraving from Christopher Wren's 'Parentalia'.**

5. **St. Matthew's. Engraving by J. Skelton, 1814, published in George Clarke's 'Londina Ecclesiastica Illustrata' (1820). The church passage at the left is shown too wide.**

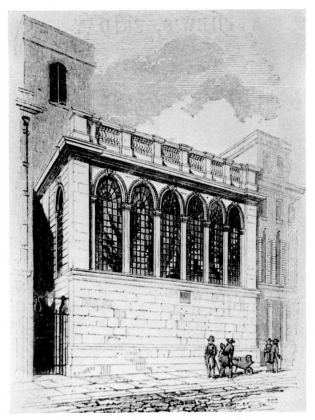

6. St. Matthew's from Friday Street. Engraving published in George Godwin and John Britton's 'Churches of London' (1839).

paid for out of parish funds, and the accounts are preserved at the Guildhall. The altar (or, rather, communion table), rails and reredos were given by a parishioner, James Smith, Esquire, and consequently the bills for these are lost. There is therefore no documentary evidence for the authorship of the reredos. Yet without doubt it was made to the approval of the Vestry, and by the same craftsmen who supplied the wainscotting, pews, font and pulpit. These were the joiner Richard Kedge, and the sculptor-carver Edward Pearce, who as we have seen was also mason for the building.

Edward Pearce (c. 1630–95) is one of the better known of the Restoration carvers, and Vertue says that he 'was much employed by Sr Chr. Wren in his Carvings & Designs'. The son of a painter of the same name, his training is obscure, but as well as sculpture and carving he practised architecture and decorative painting. His father had published a series of engravings entitled *Designs for Friezes* in 1640,[1] which Pearce re-issued in 1668 and again about 1680 (Fig. 9). At Sudbury Hall, Derbyshire (now a National Trust Property) Pearce made panelling and the magnificent staircase balustrade in pine and limewood, c. 1675 (Fig. 10). He was mason at four Wren churches, and he supplied carved woodwork for six of them. Hardly any of this now remains. St. Benet Fink was demolished

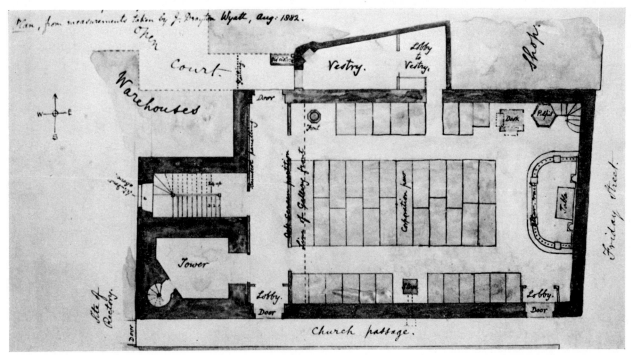

7. St. Matthew's. Surveyor's plan, dated August 1882, just prior to demolition. The church had been reseated in 1862 (Guildhall Library).

8. John Crowther: Interior of St. Matthew's, dated November 1881. Watercolour ($7\frac{1}{4} \times$ 10 cm), made after the church was declared redundant. The Churchwardens' pew is at the back (Guildhall Library; Chadwick-Healey Collection).

9. Edward Pearce senior (d. 1658). Two designs for friezes, from a set, originally published in 1640; reissued 1668 and about 1680. They may have been intended for painting.

10. Edward Pearce (*c.* 1630–1695). Carved overdoor, 1675–6, at Sudbury Hall, Derbyshire.

11. Herbert Horne. Interior of St. Matthew's, seen from the gallery. One of several monochrome drawings made in 1881–2. (National Monuments Record).

12. The East End. Detail from Crowther's water-colour (Fig. 8).

in 1843, St. Matthew Friday Street in 1884; and four churches, including the splendid interiors at St. Lawrence Jewry, were burnt out in the blitz of 1940.

When St. Matthew's was opened the furnishing was virtually complete (though Pearce continued to receive minor payments for work until 1687). For the marble font he charged £23; for carving its oak cover, £4.16s, the joiner having already supplied the cover uncarved for £3 (Fig. 13). The joiners made the 'pulpit and type (*i.e.* sounding board) and stares' by January 1685 for £55, and Pearce's bill 'for ye Carving of ye Pullpit & Tipe by estimation' was £30 (Fig. 14). These were not high prices, and by comparison with other City churches the St. Matthew's pulpit was simple. The carving surrounds parquetry panels. We have no record of how the 'type' looked, for at some point it was removed, perhaps because it obstructed the light; but it can hardly have been so large as some which survive, as for instance at St. Stephen Walbrook, because there was not much room.

The only reference to the altar-piece in Pearce's accounts clearly refers to a small improvement to the completed work:

(October 1685) for 3 foo of leaves & lace
for ye Rerdoss per 1s. foo: 00: 03: 0

The earliest and fullest description of the reredos comes from Edward Hatton's *New View of London* (1708), and since this tells of its original decoration it may be quoted in full:

The [Altar-piece is] adorned with 2 fluted Columns,

13. Marble font and oak cover, carved by Edward Pearce for St. Matthew's, now at St. Andrew by the Wardrobe.

14. The Pulpit, made by Woodroffe and Johnson, and carved by Edward Pearce; now at St. Andrew by the Wardrobe.

and Entablature, and Compass-pediment, of the *Corinthian* order; [in] the Intercolumniations are the Commandments in gilt frames, and done in gold Letters on Black under a Cherubim; without the Columns, are the Lord's Prayer and Creed done in Black on Gold, each under a small triangular pediment, where is placed on 2 shields J.R. and the Queen's Arms ... and the whole Altar-piece has Enrichments of 4 Lamps; also Festoons, Fruit, Leaves, &c, all of oak; ...

The decoration was slightly modified later. A bill from Joseph Rowe in 1766, when extensive repairs were carried out to the church, mentions 'painting the Cherubim heads, Curtain & Gilding the 2 Shields at the Altar, £1.7.0'. The heads and 'curtain' may refer to the pulpit and 'type'.

When the last Rector, Mr. Sparrow Simpson, made alterations in 1862, he quite transformed the Altar-piece by gilding, as the *City Press* recorded on 20 December 1862:

The Reredos is a fine specimen of wood carving and has been judiciously treated by Mr. Shaw. The prominent members of the different parts have been plentifully relieved by gilding and the commandments re-written in red on a gold ground. Before so dark & dull, it now forms a most beautiful ornament to the church. The panels of the richly carved pulpit have been discovered to be carefully inlaid, the beauty of the pattern having been concealed by repeated coats of varnish. These have been cleaned & carefully restored ...[2]

Crowther's watercolour (1881) (Fig. 8) shows the extent of the gilding, which seems to have been in two tones of gold; or perhaps some carvings were painted. The gilding included the capitals and flutings of the columns. Such liberal expenditure seems misjudged, for the church had only twenty-two more years of existence.

The altar-piece was made to stand against a flat wall, and its three sections were in the same vertical plane. The old drawings show how much of the original carving has been lost. However, there remain two of the four lamp finials, the palm and laurel branches in the frieze, and the mouldings round the Commandments; and, most prominent, the Cherub's head, two fine cartouches, and the flower festoons. The upper parts of the festoons are

15. St. Matthew's demolished. From 'The Graphic', 12 March 1884.

carved in full relief, but the vertical drops are applied to the grounds and are closer to half-relief. Horne's drawing of 1881–82 (Fig. 11) is inaccurate, showing the side drops only about half their true length.

Edward Pearce was certainly among the finest carvers of his day, but his reputation has understandably been eclipsed by Grinling Gibbons. Gibbons's luxuriant reredos at St. James Piccadilly, set up in 1684, shows an artistry of a different order, but it was carried out in the tractable material of limewood. In these festoons, Pearce developed the brittle, airy style that he had used at Sudbury Hall ten years earlier, and here his achievement was to execute the natural forms with extraordinary delicacy and vitality in the difficult medium of oak (Fig. 16).

The destruction of St. Matthew's was lamented at the time, but is only a small part of a long melancholy story. During the nineteenth century commercial interests were steadily displacing the resident population, and some fifty City churches within the old walls were embarrassing City and Church alike. Far from being regarded as valuable

treasuries, Wren's churches, with their urbane architecture and craftsmanship, were out of keeping with the liturgical spirit of the times. The authorities were determined to remove many of them, and the only problem was how this could be done so as best to serve both the established interests. Three Wren churches were demolished (1781, 1831 and 1843) for new buildings or roads. But the 'final solution' came with the *Union of Church Benefices Act*, passed by Parliament in 1860. This affected other old cities besides London, and allowed funds to be raised for new parishes in the expanding suburbs by demolishing churches in under-populated urban districts. By 1938 the Act had resulted in sixteen Wren churches being removed from the City, and there were plans to destroy at least eighteen more. Hitler's *Blitzkrieg* went far towards completing what had been intended during the previous hundred years.

The first Wren church demolished under the Act was St. Benet Gracechurch Street, in 1867. By 1881 when St. Matthew's was declared redundant, six more had disappeared. Meanwhile, protection societies were formed and the R.I.B.A. was

16. **The central section of the Altarpiece in its present state.**

17. One of the doorcases flanking the reredos.

expected would be a moated site with, originally, a hall where the lord's family might stay on progress, and which would later be supplemented by extensions to meet rising standards of living.

A description of the manorhouse in 1376[2] confirms this. There was a 'hall of ancient fashion', with domestic offices (pantry, buttery, kitchen and bakehouse), and residential extensions (a chamber for the lord, a chapel and a 'noricerie' and a 'garite'); the whole was surrounded with a mud wall, in which were three gates, the chief having a watch-tower and drawbridge (implying a moat). The building material of the hall is not given. As regards the subsidiary buildings, their roofs were of tile which was in bad repair; and their timbers

were in a like state; it is not clear whether these buildings were timber-framed. The mud wall round the whole was 'altogether razed and destroyed'. Farm buildings included a barn, dovecote, and water-mill. Two factors probably contributed to this lack of upkeep: by this time periodic visits from the lord's family may have diminished or ceased; moreover, in 1376 only a generation had elapsed since the Black Death.

Where was this manorhouse? In 1973 a moated site, thought to be of Danish origin,[3] was excavated at the east end of the village, not far from the former mill. Excavation showed that it was in occupation in the twelfth and thirteenth centuries.[4] The present manorhouse is at the west end of the

2. **Window on the upper floor of the stable, looking south towards the church.**

3. **Roof timbers in the stable at Willington.**

village,[5] as are the buildings owned by the National Trust. If the manorial buildings were removed from one end of the village to the other, how and why did the change take place? It will be noted that the recent excavation did not find material later than the thirteenth century, although it would be unwise to assume that the small trial trench revealed every possible fact about the moated site.

Absentee ownership continued in the later Middle Ages, and if there was a motive for the lord to build a fine house at Willington, we have no clue to it. John de Mowbray, Earl of Nottingham and of Norfolk, born in 1444, succeeded in 1461 as an only son, and left an infant daughter Anne, who was married to one of the princes in the Tower, whom she predeceased. The Mowbray estates passed (after temporary confiscation following the battle of Bosworth) to the Howards. Thomas Howard, Duke of Norfolk, died in 1524. It was his son who in 1529 sold Willington to John Gostwick.

Gostwick[6] was a local man, whose ancestors had served as bailiffs in the fourteenth century, and who himself had risen in the service of Wolsey (subsequently of Henry VIII), and also had business ventures in the city. Leland,[7] passing this way soon afterwards in the 1530s, noted that the 'old manor place' was 'clean down', 'but the place is notably seen where it was'. 'Clean down' would seem to imply that nothing of the walls was left (Bedford castle, demolished three centuries previously, was also 'clean down'), but there must have been enough visible evidence to attract his attention.

A defensive moat was no longer needed, and a new site would facilitate creating a deer park. Leland does not mention a park, but its existence can be deduced from the fact that in 1535 Gostwick sent two sides of red deer to Thomas Cromwell (presents of venison were routine, and we hear of this only because mild weather endangered its keeping).[8] The house was, says Leland, 'a sumptuous building of brick and timber', brick being then a material of recent popularity. Leland is sparing with his adjectives; his more usual ones are 'fair' and 'pretty', and not even these are applied to Compton Wynyates; perhaps Gostwick's mansion was equal to Sir William Compton's, if not superior. Details of it are given in the will (1547) of Gostwick's brother and eventual heir, William; they include the 'king's chamber' where 'King Henry VIII of famous memory' of late lay (1541), inner chamber, presence chamber, hall, parlour, chapel, and a number of other rooms. The extent of the mansion (of which remaining brickwork in the walls of the present garden gives some indication) may have been at least three times that of the present house.

It would be reasonable to move in addition the site of the home farm, and place it, not beside the mansion, but on the edge of the park. Why however, when the house was of brick, are the farm buildings of stone, and where did Gostwick get his stone? In this connection, it is worth noting that he also altered the church. An inscription dated 1541, at the juncture of the chancel and what is known as the Gostwick chapel, says 'hoc opus fieri fecit'.

There seem to be two possible reasons for using stone for the farm buildings. One is that at this time stone quarries (for instance at Barnack in Northants.) were still working, and stone was cheaper than brick. The other is that he had access to used stone nearby. Between 1538 and 1540 he was concerned in the dissolution of four religious houses in the county, including Greyfriars at Bedford, and Newnham Priory. The latter was situated beside the river Ouse, just outside Bedford, and the river flows within half a mile of Willington church. It is known that Gostwick took lead from Greyfriars to Willington.[9]

Sir John, who was knighted in 1541, died in 1545,

4.   The fireplace in the upper room. The square panel of glass protects a (possibly authentic) signature of John Bunyan.

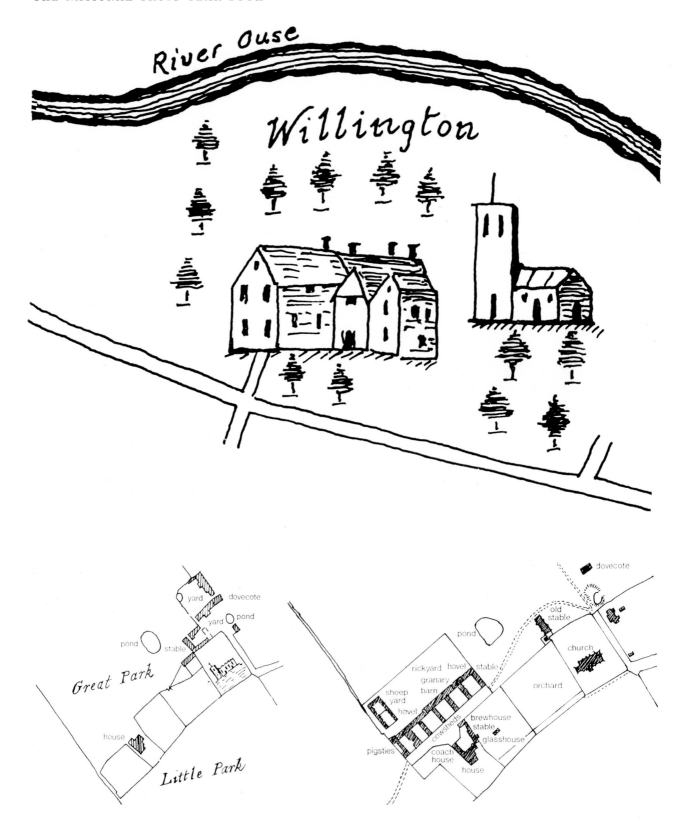

5. Three maps of Willington taken from surveys of 1736 (top), 1779 (left) and 1901 (right).

6. Rev. David Powell, the dovecote and barn at Willington, dated 1811, from Powell's topographical collections in the British Museum.

leaving an extensive estate, partly in nearby villages, partly outside the county. He had also bought a moiety of the barony of Bedford. Had he been followed by descendants, the family might have risen to further rank and power. But his son, to whom he had written advice on estate management, emphasizing the importance of a good bailiff (and indicating a preference for bachelors) died in the same year.[10] Gostwick's brother William, who died in 1549, left a son 'of little understanding'. The family continued at Willington till 1731, when their estate was sold, becoming in 1774 the property of the Dukes of Bedford.

Village tradition says that much of the Gostwick mansion ('forty rooms') was burnt or pulled down. The remainder was converted to a farmhouse, apparently before the Duke's estate accounts begin. The 1779 map shows the park enclosed: Great Park appears as a field north of the house; to the south, the name Little Park continued until the present century. Up-to-date farm buildings, however, were not planned till 1850. The Bedfordshire Architectural and Archaeological Society[11] pleaded with the Duke not to demolish the old dovecote, stable and barn; the barn was in too bad a state, but the other two were saved. Of the barn, a sketch survives in the British Museum in Powell's Topographical Collections[12] and shows it partly of stone, partly of brick and timber. Its materials were used as foundations for the new farm buildings. When in 1943–48 alterations to these involved exposing the foundations, some stone was found to have mouldings on a scale which suggested massive work, including sections of nave pillars, as well as smaller mouldings such as coping stones.

Historical Conclusion

It seems certain the buildings were Sir John Gostwick's farm buildings. Pigeons were valued for food, and a letter survives from him to Thomas Cromwell, sending him two dozen pigeons.[13] A good stable was a necessity for a man involved in public affairs and able to entertain the king. Why, however, has it living quarters on the upper floor, to which access was by ladder? Such accommodation would seem to be for a responsible employee, yet one not entitled to the refinements a gentleman would expect, for instance the bailiff of the home farm: 'some honest man to have the charge of your husbandry'. It is probable that the Willington bailiff had responsibility also for the estate in the nearby parishes of Cople, Goldington, Ravensden and Renhold, and hence was a man of some importance. Did he occupy the upper room with the fireplace, while the grooms slept in the larger room adjoining, and the horses were accommodated below? The former east doorway, now blocked, gave access to the farmyard. The bailiff would be well placed to intercept would-be poachers of the park deer. He and the grooms probably took their meals with the other staff at the great house. Here the annual consumption of mutton alone was 60 wethers (rams),[14] and if we infer a like amount of beef, pork, poultry, game and venison, a fair-sized retinue is indicated.

To what extent, if at all, did Gostwick use monastic stone? His neighbour at Hinchingbrooke a little later in similar circumstances supplied himself with a gatehouse by removing that of Ramsey Abbey.[15] At Willington, were the window-frames and the fireplace brought from Newnham Priory? If he did thus bring his materials from elsewhere, he must have had sufficient architectural appreciation (and sufficient wealth) to preserve in his new farm buildings something of the beauty of those from which they came.

Is the problem merely that the splendour of Gostwick's farm buildings puzzles us because they are residuary survivals? Could we imagine the house of Russell extinct and forgotten, and at Woburn only such outbuildings surviving as were there at Queen Elizabeth's visit in 1572, those outbuildings might well be impressive in their own right. In this view, the splendour of the stable is not an indication that it has been down-graded from a gentleman's residence; rather, stable and dovecote point to the 'sumptuousness' of Gostwick's vanished mansion.

The Tudor period provided opportunities for new men, and Bedfordshire shows a sharp contrast in the later fortunes of two such families. Sir William Russell's descendants, partly by fortunate marriages, increased their estate and rose to be Dukes of Bedford, producing in later generations figures as celebrated as the 4th Earl, the drainer of the fens, Lord John Russell, of the Reform Bill, and Bertrand Russell, the philosopher. Sir John Gostwick's only son died, and his brother's heirs included no notable men, while in less than two centuries their estate was sold and the family petered out.

Notes

[1] *Victoria County History of Bedfordshire*, London, 1912, vol. III, p. 262.

[2] *Calendar of Inquisitions Miscellaneous*, vol. III, pp. 392–3.

[3] *Victoria County History of Bedfordshire*, London, 1904, vol. I, pp. 282–4.

[4] J. Hassall, 'Excavations at Willington, 1973', *Bedfordshire Archaeological Journal*, vol. X, 1975, pp. 25–40. The finds included pottery (bowls, jugs, cooking pots), iron (nails, spurs, knives) and animal bones (cattle, sheep, birds, rabbits, pigs, deer, dog).

[5] The first surviving map (Russell collection, Bedford Record Office), is 1779, and shows the road from the village terminating at the north-east corner of the churchyard, leading into a group of farm buildings. Access to the manorhouse was through the park from the main road, as shown by a still surviving cart road.

[6] A thorough study of the Gostwicks by the late H. P. R. Finberg was published by the Bedfordshire Historical Record Society in their vol. XXXVI.

[7] L. T. Smith (ed.), 1907, vol. I, pp. 101–2.

[8] Finberg, op. cit., p. 64.

[9] Finberg, op. cit., p. 69.

[10] A. G. Dickens, 'Estate and Household Management in Bedfordshire, c. 1540', *Bedfordshire Historical Record Society*, vol. XXXVI, p. 38.

[11] Godber, *History of Bedfordshire*, Bedford, 1969, p. 525.

[12] British Museum, Add. MSS. 17456, f.44.

[13] Finberg, op. cit., p. 61.

[14] Dickens, op. cit., p. 43.

[15] N. Pevsner, *Bedfordshire and the County of Huntingdon and Peterborough*, 1968, p. 264, pl. 60.

The Park and Garden at Dyrham

ANTHONY MITCHELL

The name Dyrham probably derives from the Saxon *deor-hamm* meaning deer enclosure, suggesting that Dyrham, on the edge of the ancient forest of Kingswood, is among the oldest recorded deer parks in the country. It is first mentioned in the Anglo-Saxon Chronicle of the late ninth century recording the decisive battle of Deorhamm in 577 whereby the West Saxons captured Bath, Cirencester and Gloucester and divided the Welsh Britons from their allies in the South West.[1]

According to Leland[2] the 'meane howse' of the Russels, the medieval lords of the manor, was rebuilt by two generations of the Denys family and in 1511 Sir William Denys obtained a licence from Henry VIII to empark 500 acres with right of free-warren. This is twice the present size of the park, which must then have extended along the Cotswold escarpment to the South, according to the field names on the 1689 estate map. On Christopher Saxton's map of Gloucestershire, in 1577, Dyrham is shown as one of some twenty deer parks. The Wynter family acquired the property in 1571 and James I granted Sir George Wynter a licence in 1620 to empark and stock lands in the manors of Dyrham and Hinton. These documents can be seen in the house and vividly suggest the noble practice, dating from medieval times, of harbouring and managing deer for food in winter and for the chase, otherwise a Royal prerogative in the forests.[3]

Following his marriage to Mary Wynter in 1686, William Blathwayt, the perfect professional (and certainly penpushing) bureaucrat of his age, 'Secretary of War, Clerk of the Council etc., having raised himself by his industry from very moderate circumstances . . . a very proper, handsome person, very dextrous in business . . .',[4] gained possession of Dyrham on the death of his father-in-law in 1689. He immediately commissioned a survey of the estate by Christopher Jacob (Fig. 3), which has recently come to light again.[5] The acreage of the whole estate, about 1,700 acres, is not very different

from that of 2,097 acres when the Blathwayts finally sold it (without the park and village) in 1974. The old Tudor house of the Denys family, long a matter for speculation, is clearly drawn and, whether or not altered by the Wynters, resembles the existing house of Syston, three miles away near Pucklechurch, built by the Denys's after they left Dyrham in 1571.[6] The approach is from the west and a garden of three roods and 27 perches is shown on the east and north-east. The old disposition of the streams and ponds is particularly interesting. There is a large pond on the east beyond the garden from which, and from two streams as now, the water flowed between the house and the stable courts in a canal or moat, then ran into another pond on the south-west (indicated in Kip and still existing as a small pool fed by fresh springs) before falling into the two mill ponds or fishponds, which are therefore certainly older than the present house. These last are flanked on both sides by orchards. The alternative derivation for the name Dyrham is the British *dwr* meaning water (favoured by Atkyns) and in the drought of the exceptional summer of 1976 the mysterious flow of water under the house never abated, nor were the ponds ever low or stagnant. The Deer Park was only seventy-eight acres and a small lodge is shown between it and the Warren, where the deer park buildings are today (top left of Fig. 5.)

William Blathwayt's celebrated transformation of this scene between 1691 and about 1704 is very well documented by the letters and accounts in the Dyrham archives in the Gloucestershire Record Office[7] and accurately portrayed, indeed immortalized, in Kip's engraving published in Sir Robert Atkyns' *Ancient and Present State of Glocestershire* in 1712 (Fig. 4). John Povey's letter[8] of December 1700 describes in some detail the fountains in the canal garden and on the west side of the house all working impressively, though not wholly finished; yet Blathwayt's letters to his agent

1. Dyrham Park, Avon. The site of the Water Garden.

2. The ancient herd of fallow deer at Dyrham in 1976.

3. **The Estate Map of 1689 made for William Blathwayt by Christopher Jacob.**

'Cozen Watkins' as late as 1704 complain of difficulties in the laying of water pipes for the fountains and delays with the mason Philip West's work in finishing the stonework in the garden and getting his accounts together. (Evidently nothing much has changed in nearly three hundred years with Gloucestershire stonemasons).

The garden on the east with its parterres, terraces, canal and wilderness, which all returned to parkland at the end of the eighteenth century, was laid out by George London. Thomas Hurnall was the head gardener at Dyrham and his plan of the top of the canal and the niches and fountains with hydraulic explanations is shown in Fig. 6 and accords exactly with Kip, unlike 'Mr. Talmans First drought of a Cascade'[9] (Fig. 7) which, had it been built, would have been more extravagantly French and baroque. Neptune, by John Harvey of Bath, 'bigger than the life' as Switzer would have

approved but without his trident or any water, is the sole survivor of Kip's scene and today looks somewhat restored on close inspection (Fig. 8). The following extracts[10] give the flavour of Blathwayt's frequent letters to Watkins written from Whitehall towards the end of the work about 1704, though most are undated.

> Since your going away I have opend a letter from Hurnall to you full of his usual stuff and foolish complaints . . . Now for Business, I will return the Draught of ye Plott of Ground at ye end of ye Long Terras with some alterations after consulting London.

Blathwayt asked Thomas Hurnall in February to send a draft of the lines of all the pipes for the water before the stone was laid for the cascade. Thomas Hurnall replies on 5 and 9 February 1704, that they are 'opening a trench to lay the pipes to the Cascade and the Grate Neich in the Canall Garden, which

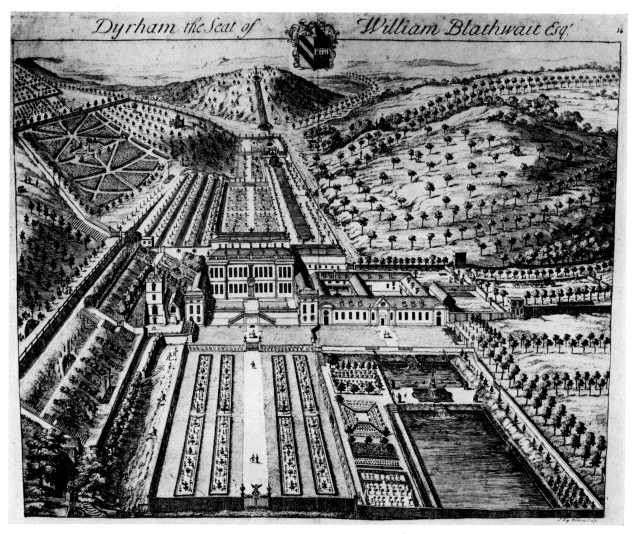

Dyrham the Seat of   *William Blathwait Esq.*

4. 'Dyrham the Seat of William Blathwayt Esq.', drawn and engraved by J. Kip and published in 1712 in Sir Robert Atkyns' 'Ancient and Present State of Glocestershire'.

hinders us from making an end of the planting in the nursery', and presumably enclosed the plan (Fig. 6). He says he is enclosing an account of the mason P. West's work, one of many existing, which he could not do before because of the work in the nursery, and says that West will now start digging for the cascade itself.

> ... you see I have changed my design for ye Long Terras. I suppose this last will be cheapest as well as most convenient and airy ... T. Hurnall writes me word he will send me up an acct: of all the work that is to be done by P. West but I would have an acct. too of all work whatsoever that is to be done this Spring and desire you would putt an end to ye difficulty and uncertainties that occasion delay. I would be glad to know in what condition the Cataract is from ye Injuries of ye Winter for a small matter would induce

me to make use of ye stone elsewhere if it be not like to endure ye Weather and ye Water.

The long terrace is clearly seen up on the left of Kip's engraving, above the wall which still exists. The cataract (as opposed to the cascade) is probably the upper waterfall in the West Garden, 'above the upper Mill Pond' for which John Harvey of Bath, who did much of the carving and sculpture at Dyrham, sent Blathwayt a draft in February 1704.

> ... after the drain I suppose West will finish ye Cataract & 'tis high time twere done.

> I hope all the fountains are filled and the Niches of the Stewpond thro out ye water

The stewpond is shown in Kip on the west of the stables and in the summer of 1976 its lines were clearly revealed by the drought and photographed. The 'noble Dutch fountain'[11] between the two millponds has also disappeared but was first noticed and measured several summers ago and its outline in the grass accords exactly with Kip. Certain drought lines in the park, on the east, showed up better than usual last year and two boundary walls of the upper parterre appeared for the first time and were photographed. They also agree with Kip and the foundations of one wall were revealed as still existing.

I don't find there is much riddance of idle fellows at Dirham. Pray tell Hurnall I Shall be sorry to find ye end of ye long terras unfinisht. That I would not have him meddle with ye earth about the pidgion House till I come.

I desire you would take care that the New Lodge fore ye Keeper and the Rough Stable be finisht as soon as maybe for I know the aversion mankind has at Dirham for *finishing* anything.

[8 July 1704] I would have Hurnall send me word by Mundays Post what Timber work of any sort he proposed to have refresht with white for this Summer and I will give him orders thereupon about it. If Mr. Oliver can shew how the Stand for Books in ye Arbors are to be made as at my Lord Fauconberg's I would have one made forthwith for that Seat Arbor which stands in ye corner of ye Wilderness to ye N.E. looking towards Bristol.

The Wilderness can be seen in Kip on the left above the terraces and this last is interesting to compare with the following from Switzer's description of Dyrham – 'I never in my whole Life did see so agreeable a Place for the sublimest Studies, as this in the Summer, and here are small Desks erected in Seats for that Purpose'.

All this can be followed with Kip before the reader (Fig. 4) and walking over the site one is surprised to discover that this apparently ambitious garden is on quite a reasonable scale, much of it

5.   **An aerial view of Dyrham in 1949, taken from near the same imaginary point as Kip's view.**

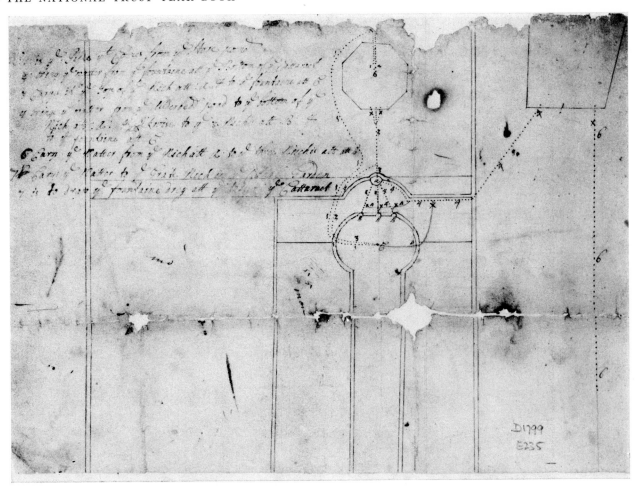

6. Thomas Hurnall's sketch plan for the head of the canal.

7. 'Mr. Talmans First drought of a cascade'. Talman was the architect of the East Front.

overlaying the Tudor garden already referred to. Its attraction and fame surely rested on its very special site, from whose dramatic slopes it would indeed have appeared 'jewel-like'.[12] One is reminded of the contours of Marly, also quite vanished, though once on a larger scale. One feels the result must have been more Italianate than most London and Wise layouts, although the axial vista and design of the parterres recall France and 'La Grand Manier'[13] rather than the 'Dutch taste' which seems to prevail on the west side with small scale topiary and kitchen gardening, and especially within the house. Dutch elements in his garden were to be expected from Blathwayt who began his career in Sir William Temple's embassy at The Hague. He must have read *Upon the Gardens of Epicurus* of 1685 (published 1692) as he possessed Temple's *Oeuvres Posthumes* (1704) as well as, for more practical purposes, John Evelyn's translation of La Quintinie's *The Compleat Gard'ner* 1693.[14]

Kip's plate, on close study, turns out to be one of his most accurate in spite of his dubious perspective. Bigland's remark[15] that Kip's view was made 'with more than his usual fidelity' is finally borne out by Stephen Switzer's long and detailed description of this layout published in 1718 in the third volume of his *Ichnographia Rustica* (printed in full in the Appendix, pp. 100–108).[16] So closely indeed does his step by step perambulation agree with Kip that one might even be tempted to suppose he had the engraving before him when he wrote of his visit 'some Years since'. Switzer is now credited with being influential in liberating garden practice from the straitjackets of formality and from 'Dutch taste', yet Dyrham seems to have exercised a curious influence on him.[17] From the preamble to his description it is clear that it was the natural situation of Dyrham with its 'beautiful Irregularity' which fascinated him, besides of course his interest in 'Hydrostaticks and Hydraulics', claiming

...that Nature has a greater Share in the Beauties I am proceeding to, than Art; not but very considerable Sums have been expended to bring these Gardens to that Perfection which I some Years since saw them in, when my affairs requir'd my Attendance on a Person of the first Rank at the Bath.

This may have been the Duke of Beaufort as Switzer visited Badminton in 1708, or perhaps Lord Bathurst for whom he worked both at Cirencester and Riskins. Coming from Badminton or Bath he would approach Dyrham from the top as he describes, whereas John Povey arrived from the

avenue on the west. Another Bath visitor was Dudley Ryder in 1715 who thought the 'cascade from a very steep hill of 224 steps, the finest in England except the Duke of Devonshire's' and 'gave the gardener five shillings and the woman that showed the house the same'.[18]

Fifty years later another estate map, by Giles Coates (Fig. 9), is undated but we have the bill for it of 1766. It shows in plan most of Kip's layout still surviving, including the canal and terraces with the wilderness, lodge and nursery above them (top left of Fig. 4). Comparison with Fig. 3 shows the nursery to have been made by Blathwayt out of the Oxe-house Tininge and it was the scene of much planting of fir trees, among others, by Hurnall. The deer park itself looks about the same size as in 1689 yet there are references to enclosing land for enlarging the park in 1666, 1670, 1690–93 and 1708, one of which provoked a prolonged dispute with the rector. The warren has been extended and planted and six maturing elm avenues are shown on the flat top of the limestone scarp, five of which, after falling about with age, finally succumbed to elm disease and were laboriously felled by the Trust in 1976. The ages of the trees in them varied with replacements but in each were recorded elm trees of about 270 years of age,[19] confirming they belonged to Blathwayt's original layout, beyond Kip's horizon (Figs. 10 and 11). Invisible from the house they escaped reconciliation 'to modern Taste'.[20] These are now being replanted with *Tilia cordata* and *Tilia platyphyllos* with help from the Countryside Commission as part of a comprehensive park planting scheme to maintain and perpetuate the landscape. A sixth avenue, traces of which were subsequently found on the ground, is shown running north-east from the deer barton, but this was already broken up by 1833 (see Fig. 14) and will not be replaced in the scheme as the landscape here does not seem suitable and its subsequent history has been taken into account.

Giles Coates' survey of 1766 does not show the cascade between the old route of the drive and Neptune and by 1779 the county historian Rudder is writing 'There is a park adjoining the gardens; but the curious waterworks, which were made at a great expense, are much neglected and going to decay'.[21] Twelve years later Bigland in 1791 says Kip's 'delineation is the more valuable as exhibiting a Bird's Eye View of the Pleasure Grounds, now reconciled to modern Taste, which were designed by Le Notre, and were the first specimen in that day, of Cascades and Jets d'Eau carried to the very

8. Neptune, by John Harvey of Bath. The original trident is missing.

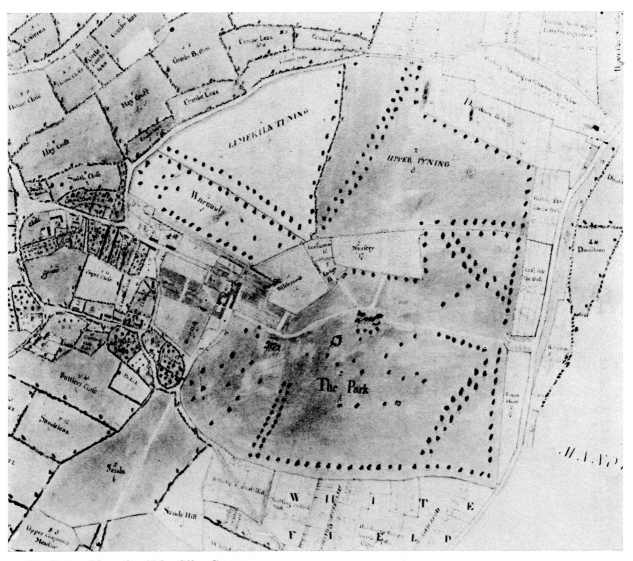

9. The Estate Map of 1766 by Giles Coates.

summit of the Hill'.[22] Repton's visit was not until 1800 and although his bill was for £66.3s. in 1801 and a balance of £24.3s. in 1803, it is not clear what he was responsible for and there is no Red Book.[23] There exists however a watercolour attributed to Repton, a 'design for the pavilion at the end of the terrace' which is difficult to site and may not have been built (Fig. 12). On the other hand a number of bills exist for the years 1798–99 from C. Harcourt-Masters,[24] the Bath surveyor, for moving a quantity of earth and for re-routing the drive along its present line south of Neptune, as shown in the plan of the park in 1833 (Fig. 14), by Thomas Weaver of Chipping Sodbury,[25] and the Ordnance Survey maps. Some dismantling beyond just abandonment must have occurred before this, as Bigland suggests, perhaps after William Blathwayt

IV inherited in 1787, although Harcourt-Masters first appears in the accounts surveying timber in 1785. A Mr. Phelps, architect, and a Mr. Gray, surveyor, were consulted in 1787 and 1790.[26] A colour wash drawing (Fig. 13) in Mr. Justin Blathwayt's possession, which appears to be post-Coates and Bigland but pre-Harcourt-Masters shows the park clumped with trees and indeed 'reconciled to modern Taste'. It does not show Harcourt-Masters' rearrangement of the levels and drive with its semi-circle near the house (Fig. 14). This view seems related to another much damaged watercolour preserved in the house,[27] which also shows the familiar long lawn on the west having replaced the avenue, as it is still known (and still easily discerned in dry summers), by which John Povey approached in 1700. The avenue is not

10. An Elm Avenue 'from the Whitfield End', photographed in 1908.

11. The adjacent Avenue before felling in 1976.

shown on the 1766 survey either (Fig. 9). The ponds still have straight sides. Old trees have been cut and the timber yard appears to have been already established south of the stables, perhaps by William Blathwayt IV to destroy some of his great grandfather's avenues near the house which would have been nearly a hundred years old.

The first William Blathwayt planted exotic trees from the American colonies which he administered such as Virginia pine, sassafras, tulip trees and Virginia flowering oaks, and panelled rooms in the house with cedar from South Carolina and the hard-grained black walnut from Virginia. There are still fine, but much later, specimens of *Liriodendron tulipifera*, *Quercus rubra* (*Q. borealis maxima*) and *Juglans nigra* in the park near the house, besides the large pair of London planes in front of the orangery which Mr. Alan Mitchell dates not much earlier than about 1800, or Harcourt-Masters' time. Limes are difficult to date, but one in the park is as old as the house and the anciently pleached ones in the church walk could possibly even be those drawn by Kip in their youth.

Thomas Hurnall, the head gardener, visited George London whenever he came to Longleat to obtain seeds. He also bought for £2.6s.10d. from 'Ja: Fuller att ye Orange Tree in ye Strand: March ye 3d 1692' Norway fir cones, Silver fir, Scotch fir and Cyprus seeds, 'Phillirea or Alla-turnus, Piracantha and Yew berries, Juniper, Althea ffrutex, Spanish Broome, Dutch Savoy, Pott Mariorum, ffrench Sorrell, Clary, English Thyme, Hysop, Chervill, Matted Pinke, Sweet William and Red and white Valerian seeds', as well as spending two shillings 'ffor a Large Garden Lyne'.[28] Most of these are more suitable for perpetuation today in the garden on the west of the house.

In September 1693 five men were employed for 'making of Holes for Trees in ye Park'[29] which is just what the Trust is doing at present to replant the elm avenues with lime, but using one man with a hole-driller. Hurnall in 1704 was busy planting phillireas and hollies along walls and near the house including some 'stript hollys'. He writes to Blathwayt for urgent instructions about 'ye fences for ye Firr trees' in February 1704 and enclosed a drawing (Fig. 15) which Blathwayt returned ordering three-sided tree-guards, rather than four-sided, the cheaper alternative.[30] In his letter Hurnall suggests paying 8d. or 9d. each, more than the usual '6d. per fence for all those he makes for ye forrist trees, but yt those about ye firr trees may be

'Design for the pavilion at the end of the Terrace at Dyrham Park. Somersets. to be built of Bath Stone'

'Ground Plan of the same whether built with Stone or Wood.'

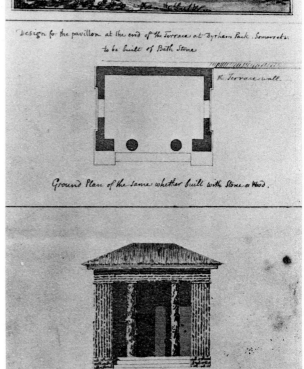

'The same plan may suit this building of wood covered with Bark of trees.'

12. Repton's 'Design for the pavilion at the end of the terrace at Dyrham Park'.

hansome . . .'.[31] The tree guards being made today are costed at £18 each.

Blathwayt's great grandson also employed Harcourt-Masters in 1798 to 'mark out the plantations' and to 'dispose and plant trees'. Varieties ordered in some quantity in January 1800 from Miller and Sweet near St. Michael's Hill, Bristol, include '25 Strong Limes, 15 ditto Syca-mores, 25 ditto Planes, 10 ditto Horse Chestnuts, 25 ditto English Elms, 110 Large picked spruce firs, 100 Beech, 50 Limes, 50 English Elms, 40 Oaks, 50 Horse Chestnuts, 25 Hornbeam, 50

13. Colour wash drawing of the park and garden, perhaps of the 1790s.

Sycamores, 50 Planes and 30 Spanish Chestnuts'. All these (except the spruce) are probably represented by living specimens of this age today and the areas where they are still to be found are well shown on the 1833 park plan (Fig. 14). Another smaller order survives for March of the same year including 10 hornbeams and 14 Spanish chestnuts, a weeping willow and two Lombardy poplars.[32]

All this was going on while Repton was still planning his first visit in September of the same year, 1800, and he could not have visited Dyrham before 1791. There are two drawings in the house dated 1821 by J. West which show a picturesque Dyrham from both the east and the west (Figs. 17 and 18). The lithograph by Hullmandel after Wilkinson (Fig. 16) might be dated about 1840, and shows a cedar plantation framing the house (as on the 1833 plan) and the best known of many

distant views from the park. Four of these old cedars still happily survive, and, like the copper beech and the picturesque leaning ilexes[33] in the garden might perhaps be Repton's work, although the cedars may not have been planted until the 1820s or later, when they became generally available and fashionable.[34] The planting activities of Colonel Blathwayt, who was energetic in other ways at Dyrham from 1839–71, have not yet been studied, but the Austrian pine and the Lucombe oak in the park near the house date from his time.

Victorian photographs of the park and elm avenues as well as of the nineteenth century appearance of the garden, a few as early as the 1870s,[35] show a mature, much loved scene which the family did nothing very much within living memory to perpetuate, at least not since the death of R. W. Blathwayt in 1936. A photograph of one of

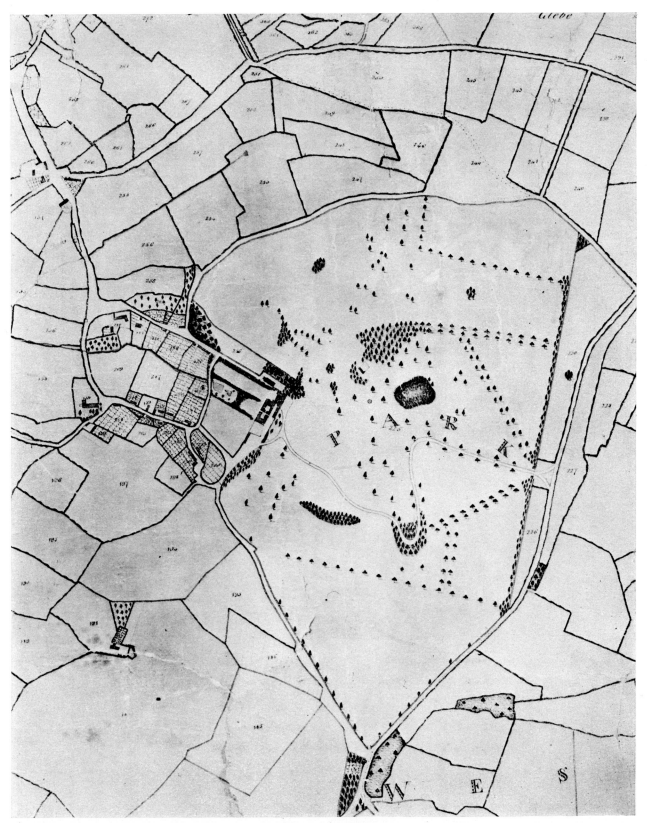

14.   A Plan of the Park in 1833 after the enclosure of the Whitefield on the South and the Upper field on the North, also showing Harcourt-Masters' new drive and plantations.

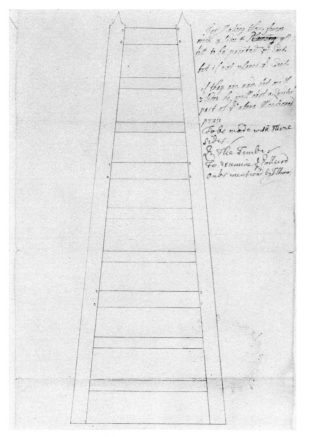

15. Thomas Hurnall's sketch for a tree-guard, 1704

the elm avenues is dated 1908 and inscribed 'from the Whitfield end' (Fig. 10). Between 1800 and 1804 the White Field on the south of the park and the Upper Field on the north were enclosed, and forty-four acres of the White Field and seventeen and a half acres of the Upper Field were added to the park, as can be seen by comparing the plans of 1766 and 1833 (Figs. 9 and 14). Both the remains of this elm avenue running south-west from the lodge and the L-shaped boundary line of ancient elms on the north-east near Badminton Doors were felled in 1976 and were part of Blathwayt's original planting. Thus the deer park finally assumed its present familiar shape.

Kip shows plenty of duck on the millponds but unfortunately no deer in the park – he was clearly more interested in the garden than the park – though in his engraving of Badminton herds of fallow deer and red deer can be seen separately enclosed between the enormous radial avenues. In December 1704 William Blathwayt received a gift of deer from Badminton[36] and lists of deer in the park in 1709–10[37] give totals of fifty-five brace. Nearly two hundred years later in 1892 the fallow deer numbered 120[38] and in recent years the herd has normally been at about this number. They are a healthy light-coloured strain, presumably of great antiquity, and the Trust is fortunate to have expert

16. Hullmandel's lithograph of Dyrham Park about 1840 showing the cedar plantation.

17 and 18.   Two Picturesque drawings of Dyrham by J. West 1821.

19. Photograph of the children of Richard Vesey Blathwayt in the garden, in about 1875.

20. The wall and fountain below the long terrace in 1903, shown in Kip (cf. Fig. 29).

advice from the British Deer Society for a constructive management policy. Towards the end of the last century the writer of 1892 describes the park

as well wooded with 'fine Dutch avenues of old elms' and having 'hilly and undulating plains, very picturesque'.

Notes

1 B. Thorpe ed. *Anglo-Saxon Chronicle* (Rolls Series 1861, vol. II, p. 17). According to the text the battle occurred 'at the place which is called Deorham'. If it was known as 'the deer enclosure' to the militarily victorious Saxons, as well as the Chronicler of 300 years later, the question arises, when were the deer enclosed? Brian Smith suggests that it might have been a Romano-British enclosure and Dyrham would certainly be an excellent, typical, Cotswold site for a Roman villa near Bath.

2 Leland's *Itinerary* part 10, quoted by John Kenworthy-Browne, *Dyrham Park*, National Trust guide book, fourth edition, 1975, p. 35. A good account of the garden and park is on pp. 29–33.

3 see John Patten, 'How the Deer Parks Began', *Country Life*, 16 September 1971, pp. 660–662.

4 John Evelyn's *Diary* 18 June 1688, ed. G. S. de Beer, Oxford 1959. Quoted in the Dyrham Park guide book, p. 41.

5 I am indebted to Justin Blathwayt for bringing me the two estate maps of 1689 and 1766 before he left Dyrham and placing them on permanent loan to the Trust (together with a third map of Blathwayt lands in Langridge, Lansdown and Weston).

6 see David Verey, *The Buildings of England, Gloucestershire*, vol. 2., ed. N. Pevsner, Harmondsworth 1970, p. 338.

7 G.R.O., D1799. The Blathwayt family papers, deposited in 1961, have been catalogued by the Gloucestershire County Archivist Brian S. Smith, whose Wednesday evening archive classes in the Record Office I have much enjoyed attending. The Dyrham Park archives formed the basis of Mark Girouard, 'Dyrham Park, Gloucestershire', *Country Life*, 15 and 22 February 1962.

8 G.R.O., D1799/E240, quoted in Dyrham Park guide book, p. 50.

9 Drawings Collection, R.I.B.A., London, G2/24. The inscription quoted is in Blathwayt's hand and Talman has also written on the back 'for Mr. Blathwayt'.

10 G.R.O., D1799. These are taken from letters in E235, E244 and E245, as also Hurnall's plan.

11 Stephen Switzer, *Ichnographia Rustica*, vol. III 1718, quoted in John Dixon Hunt and Peter Willis, *The Genius of the Place, the English Landscape Garden 1620–1820*, London 1975, p. 158. This description of Dyrham was first brought to our attention a few years ago by John Harris, whose discoveries are continuously illuminating.

12 John Kenworthy-Browne. Dyrham Park guide book, p. 30.

13 see William Brogden, 'Stephen Switzer "La Grand Manier"' in *Furor Hortensis* ed. Peter Willis, Edinburgh 1974.

14 *Catalogue of Books in the Library at Dyrham Park, Gloucestershire*, compiled by W. E. Blathwayt, Bath 1905. I am grateful to Marshall Sisson for drawing my attention to the existence of the latter important horticultural escape.

15 Ralph Bigland, *Historical, Monumental and Genealogical Collections, Relative to the County of Gloucester*, London 1791, vol. 1, p. 533, quoted in Dyrham Park guide book, p. 53.

16 Switzer, op. cit.

17 Brogden, op cit.

18 *The Diary of Dudley Ryder*, 1715–1716, transcribed by William Matthews, London 1939, p. 248, quoted in Dyrham Park guide book, p. 51.

19 I am grateful to Alan Mitchell for dating trees in the elm avenues during felling in the wet autumn of 1976. Some of the largest and the last to die from elm disease were wych elms, referred to several times in Blathwayt's letters.

20 Dyrham Park Planting Plan 1976 by my colleague Bill Wright.

21 Samuel Rudder, *A new History of Gloucestershire*, Cirencester 1779, p. 427, quoted in Dyrham Park guide book, p. 53.

22 Bigland, op. cit.

23 G.R.O., D1799/C171.

24 G.R.O., D1799/A160, A161, Anthony Wherry, formerly assistant Gloucestershire county archivist, drew my attention to these bills for exhibition at Dyrham which reveal Harcourt-Masters' role in the park.

25 G.R.O., D1799/P7, 'Plan of the Manors of Dyrham and Hinton and West Lyttleton' scale 13.3 in. to 1 mile.

26 G.R.O., D1799/A147 and A150. I am grateful to Paul Kendrick for much help with the preliminary consideration of the documents on the ground and many original suggestions.

27 I am grateful to Edward Croft-Murray and Mr. Harding of the British Museum for the rescue of this very damaged drawing, of more interest as a record than a work of art.

28 G.R.O., D1799/A102.

29 G.R.O., D1799/A103.

30 G.R.O., D1799/E235(37).

31 G.R.O., D1799/E244.

32 G.R.O., D1799/A162.

33 Illustrated in Hugh Johnson, *The International Book of Trees*, Mitchell Beazley 1973, p. 157. Also the fine, grafted, manna ash, p. 238.

34 Alan Mitchell – the cedar near the house is 115 feet high and 18 feet 2 inches in girth. The copper beech is 84 feet high and 16 feet 11 inches wide. The Austrian pine is 85 feet high and 13 feet 9 inches wide and the Lucombe oak, grafted onto a Turkey oak, is estimated at over a hundred years of age.

35 I am grateful to David Johnson for finding the photographs of about 1875 and Mrs. Cecily Grinling for cataloguing the collection in the house. They may yet identify the artists behind the cameras.

36 G.R.O., D1799/C167.

37 G.R.O., D1799/E45.

38 Joseph Whitaker, *A Descriptive List of the Deer-Parks and Paddocks of England*, 1892, p. 61.

Appendix: Description of the Garden at Dyrham from Stephen Switzer's 'Ichnographia Rustica', Vol. III, 1718, pp. 113-127

Note

Kip's well-known engraving of the gardens at Dyrham published in 1712 (Fig. 4) was long thought too elaborate and ambitious ever to have been achieved. But John Harris's rediscovery of this detailed description of the layout by Switzer, published only six years after Kip's view, and subsequent research into William Blathwayt's papers, has confirmed practically every square inch of the engraving, and greatly expanded our knowledge of the whole garden. Switzer's description is particularly valuable for those parts of the layout in the middle distance of Kip's view, where the amount of detail is necessarily restricted (compare for instance Switzer's description of the Second Parterre and Cascade with Figs. 24 and 25), but the whole chapter stands as one of the most fascinating and graphic contemporary descriptions of any great Baroque garden, perhaps equalled only by Dr. Walter Harris's famous description of William III's gardens at Het Loo, published in 1699.

Because of the rarity of Switzer's book, it has seemed worthwhile to reproduce his full description here, illustrated by details from Kip's engraving, itself recently reprinted by the National Trust and now on sale at Dyrham.

Chapter VIII, Section IX. A Description of a beautiful Rural Garden

Before I quit my agreeable and entertaining Subject of Designs in general, I cannot omit giving a particular Description of a *Rural Garden*, which tho' not equally extensive, yet perhaps equally beautiful to most we have in *England*, notwithstanding the happy Possessor bears no higher Character than that of a private Gentleman.*

I have been a great many Pages in treating of Situations, which a Man would always willingly chuse, tho' it is rarely in his Power: I therefore hope this Description will be the more acceptable, as it contains matter of Fact, and is no way chimerical; and when 'tis consider'd, that Nature has a greater Share in the Beauties I am proceeding to, than Art; not but very considerable Sums have been expended to bring these Gardens to that Perfection which I some Years since saw them in, when my Affairs requir'd my Attendance on a Person of the first Rank at the *Bath*.

To describe the Situation of the Seat in general is a Task of Difficulty; the best Account I can give of it in a few Words, is, that 'tis a beautiful Irregularity, here a Dale, there a Mount, here a winding Valley, there a purling Stream, &c. And indeed the Quantity of Water which abounds here and plentifully supplies the Waterworks is found Fault with by some Persons as an Annoyance to the House, seated low; but without considering the many large and most exquisite contriv'd Drains erected for its Conveyance to distant Ponds.

Some injudicious Persons likewise make an Exception to the Situation of this Seat, not only for its being low and moist; but on account of it being surrounded on one Side with Hills, so as not to be discern'd 'till you come just upon it; what ever Fault this may be in the Esteem of the Generality of Mankind, I shall not pretend to determine; but I have this to offer in its Favour, that on your Approach to the House from the Hills, you are at once entertain'd with an infinite Variety of beautiful Prospects, the surprizing Pleasure whereof would have been in a great Measure lost by a remote anticipating View. And from the other Side of the House, a fine Vale of a considerable Extent is discover'd even from the first Floor, notwithstanding its being low with Respect to the Northern Side, encompass'd with aspiring Mounts.

But as it is not my Business to engage in a particular Defence of a Gentleman's Choice of Situation, (wherein Fancy always presides with the greatest of Men) I shall proceed to my particular Description; and herein first begin with the *Green-house* [Fig. 21]. To pass by the Magnificence of the Seat, the *Green-house* adjoining to it, is, I think, one of the most beautiful and commodious Piles for its Purpose, I ever saw; it is near a hundred Foot in Length, and of a proportionable Breadth and height. The Outside is built of the finest Stone, adorn'd with numerous Collumns of the finest Architecture, and the main Front neatly set off with extensive Sash Windows, in Height almost from the Bottom to the Top: You ascend five or

* Mr. Blathwayt's Gardens at Durham near the Bath in Gloucestershire.

21. **The Greenhouse at Dyrham. Designed by William Talman in 1701, and joined to the east front of the house.**

six magnificent Stone Steps to enter, where you have a large folding Glass Door: Underneath are Vaults with Stoves for Fire in the Winter, and Repositories of Garden-Tools, and the Top is surrounded with Rail and Ballister, having at proper Distances an agreeable Variety of small Statues mixt with Urns, &c. And in the Front are various Motto's in large Characters of Gold, very well adapted to so noble a Conservatory.

This *Green-house* in the Winter is replete with all Manner of fine Greens, as Oranges, Lemons, Mirtles, &c. set in the most beautiful order; several Rows of Scaffolds one above another, are erected for this Purpose, on the Topmost whereof are plac'd the most tender, but largest Plants; and the Shrubs, Flowers, &c. below, so as to make the Figure of a Slope with Walks between the whole Length, for the Gardener to examine into the Health and State of his numerous Vegetables: The Inside of the House, if I mistake not, is cas'd with Bricks, which keeps it naturally warm and healthy; there are several Stoves underneath at convenient

Distances for Firing, whereby a regular Heat is diffus'd over the whole House, and the Outside is so well guarded with Shutters in the Winter, as to disdain the Fury of the most penetrating Winds.

The Stoves being very large, especially at the East end, by a prudential displaying of them in the spring, inures the Greens to the Air so as to prepare them for a Removal to the Parterre; and when most of the hardiest Plants are expos'd Abroad, it is usual here to preserve two or three Rows of Oranges, &c. the Length of the House, which make most beautiful and fragrant Walks within Doors; and the whole House is whitewash'd, and hung round with the most entertaining Maps, Sculptures, &c. And furnish'd with fine Chairs of Cane for the Summer.

When you quit the *Green-house*, at the Foot of the Steps are plac'd two prodigious large and fine Aloes, which with their prickly, bulky Arms, high extended, appear like Giants to defend the Entrance of the Conservatory: Turning to the left you find a spacious Pavement Walk, the whole Length of the

22. **The Parterre. This and the following eight illustrations are all details from Kip's engraving of Dyrham (Fig. 4) published in 1712.**

Front of the House and *Green-house* at each End whereof are Paintings in Niches representing Statues.

To this Pavement in the Summer are carry'd Orange-Trees, Lemons, round-headed Bays &c. in Tubs, and plac'd in Rows, so as to make a most delightful Walk before the whole Front, which is continu'd on the left against the Side of a Terrace-Walk, to the upper Part of the first Parterre: The Parterre [Fig. 22] is cut into four Quarters of Grass and Gravel, of various Forms, the Borders adjoining to the principal Gravel Walk, leading to the main Door of the Front, being set off with large Pyramid Silver Hollies, Ews, &c. having painted Iron Rods with gilded Nobs for their Support, and the Center-Sides, &c. with round-headed Laurels exactly

clipt, Bays, small Pyramid Ews, &c.

Facing the Front of the *Green-house* is a running Canal of clear Water, about a hundred Yards in Length [Fig. 23], at the upper End, in an enlarg'd Circle, with a high Head of fine Stone, is a Fountain which casts Water above sixty Foot in Height, and great Variety of small Pipes playing all round which entirely fill the Circle or Head of the Canal. In this Canal several Sorts of Fish are confin'd, as Trout, Perch, Carp, &c. of a very large Size, and tho' it is deep, yet the Water is so transparent that you may easily discover the scaley Residents, even those of the smallest Dimensions: And this Canal is so very much frequented in the Summer, that the Fish will not be disturb'd at your Approach; but are almost as tame as the Swans, (two whereof continually waft themselves with Grandeur in this Canal) which will not scruple to take an uncommon Feeding from your Hands.

The Situation of the Canal is lower than the Parterre before the Body of the House, separated with Walls; that on the Left making the Parterre a Terrace, and that on the right dividing the Garden from the Park; so that it is as it were a private Garden of itself, and indeed is a most pleasant one in a hot Season: In the Walls on each Side are several Falls of Water, from Pipes and Monsters Heads to Basons, from one Bason to another, which at last empty into Streams appearing like Brooks, and these discharge themselves into the Canal: One of the Walls is fill'd with Fruit-Trees, and the other (the highest) with Ever-Greens; and of each Side the Canal are Walks of Bays, Philireas, &c. in Tubs, and two very large Silver Hollies at the End to grace the Entrance.

The Wall of the Canal is cover'd with a Coping of fine Free Stone, and so are all the Walls belonging to these Gardens. At the upper End of it are about half a dozen Stone Steps, which lead you to the second Parterre: This Parterre [Fig. 24] is of the whole Breadth of the Garden, and is finely adorn'd with round-headed Standard Laurels, pyramid Ews, &c. with Iron Rods and gilded Nobs; and the two Quarters of it, on each Side the large Walk leading to the Front-Door, are during the Summer set off with Oranges in Tubs, &c. in the Nature of an Orangery: Opposite to the Canal, is an Octagon Fountain of a considerable Extent, the Pipe in the Middle throws a large Stream of Water a very great Height; and round it there are eight large Cases or Heads facing each Side of the Octagon, with a Multitude of small Pipes very close together, which when play'd, make a very good Representation of Pillars of Water.

The End of this Parterre is fenc'd in from the Park with curious Iron Work, on Dwarf-Walls; and on Pillars between the Spikes are fix'd Variety of Heads carv'd out of fine Stone; here's a large Iron Gate beautifully Wrought, and finely painted and gilded, which lets you into the Park; after you have pass'd about twenty Yards on a Gravel Walk in the Park, you come to a noble Cataract or extended Cascade of Water [Fig. 25]; this Cascade is on a Line with the Octagon Fountain, and the Canal, and all exactly fronting the Door of the *Green-house*; it has, as I remember, near two hundred and fifty Steps to the Top, and as many Falls for the Water to descend, and it is so high, that you have several Seats erected for Resting. At the

23. **The Canal.**

24. The Second Parterre.

Bottom there is a large Oval Pond with a Fountain
in it; at the Top there is likewise the same, and in
the Middle a large and lofty Pedestal, supporting
a Neptune cut out in Stone, of large Dimensions,
with an exalted Trident in his Hand; a Whale is
represented between his Legs, discharging a great
Quantity of Water into Basons on the Heads of
Tritons, from whence it falls large Sheets to the
Pond.

At regular Distances are plac'd several small
Pipes or Fountains to the Top of the Cataract, on
the Steps which facilitate the Descent of the
Water; these Pipes, when they play, seem a Slope-
Walk of Fountains; and when the Cataract plays
at the same Time, the Weight of the Water, and
the Falls are so great, that the Noise very near
equals the Billows of a raging Sea, and may be
heard at a very great Distance: At the Bottom of
the Steps are planted two Thorns encompass'd
with Seats, which are arriv'd to a large Stature, and
being kept of a round regular Form with frequent
Clippings, make a very good Figure: There are
small Pipes which twine round the Bodies of these
Trees, and appear more like Ivy on the rough
Bark, (being painted Green) than leaden Pipes,
which on the Turn of a Cock discharge Water from
a vast Number of small Nosils in the Head of the
Trees, all round as natural as if it rain'd; and in a
cloudy Day I have been inform'd, Spectators
setting down here to rest themselves, the more
these Pipes have play'd, the closer they have em-
brac'd the Tree for Shelter, supposing it had really
rain'd, till the Gardener has convinc'd them of

25. The cascade.

their Error, after they had partaken of a sufficient Sprinkling to imprint in their Memories the pleasurable Mistake.

Between this Hill, which gives the Situation for the Cataract, and a Hill in the Park, you have a fine winding Valley of about half a Mile in Length, planted with Horse-Chesnuts [Fig. 26]; at the upper End is a fine Brake of Wood on the one Side, and on the other a large square Pond; from this Pond a small Channel is cut for the Water, which after a great many Falls from Cascades, at Length enters another Pond, so that you are never out of the agreeable Noise of a murmuring Stream. Near this Pond, at the Entrance of the Chestnut-Walk, is likewise a third Pond, of a large Extent, having in the Middle a very fine Statue and Fountain.

From hence you come back to the Garden, and mount the Terras-Walks [Fig. 27], which are several, one above another, and very beautiful; the first adjoins to the North Side of the House, so that you come from a Closet, one Pair of Stairs, immediately out upon it; and at the End of this, in the Middle of a small Slope-Garden, enclos'd with a lofty Hedge on one Side, and a high Wall on the other, is a small Statue representing *Iris*, from which a Fountain plays, and fills all that Quarter with seeming Rain, to the very great Refreshment of those Persons who frequent the Rooms facing it in a scorching Season: But to return to the Terras's; there are four in Number of a good Length one

above another before you arrive at the Top, at the Ends of which you have a Wall to separate them from the Church-yard, beautify'd with fine Paintings in Niches; except it be in one of the broadest, where you have a most commodious Summer-House, answering to a Pigeon-House on t'other Side in the Park. You ascend these Terras-Walks on large square Stone Steps, 'till you come near the Top, when you arrive at very grand and magnificent Steps, cut out in the form of a half Circle.

When you have ascended these Terras's, the first Thing which offers to your Sight, is a large Stone Statue on a handsome Pedestal, near a Wilderness, and a fine Fountain with plenty of Fish, on Ground of a more exalted Elevation than the Top of the House; from thence you proceed to two Noble Terras-Walks, each above a quarter of a Mile in Length, one for the most Part enclos'd with a very lofty Hedge, kept shorn, and a Wall with Fruit-Trees, making it a solitary Walk, and the other open and expos'd; but planted on one Side with round headed Dwarf Elms, and Firs, and Iron Rails on the other: From this Terras you have a prospect from you of about eight or ten Miles over a rich and fertile Vale, which, by Variety of Woods, Groves, and Meadows, appears like a *Rural Garden* to this stately Mansion. Here you have in View the Avenue to the House, which is full of stately Plantations, and to which you have a regular Descent or Slope planted with Dwarf

26. **The Chestnut Avenue.**

27.   The Slope Garden and Terrace Walks, showing the summerhouse at the end of the fourth terrace.

28. **The ponds and 'Dutch' fountain, with the two statues of sphinxes.**

Fruit-Trees. On the other Side of the grand
Avenue are two very large Ponds [Fig. 28], almost
cover'd with Water-Fowl, and a noble *Dutch*
Fountain between, having small Seats and Arbours
all round, and Falls of Water, which make the
Figure of a Pyramid, by descending from one
Bason to another: In the Court-Yard before the
House are two large Pedestals with Sphynxes,
finely carv'd, and the Stew-Pond; on one Side is the
Orchard, and at the End is the Kitchen-Garden.

As you proceed on the Terras Walk, you meet
with Niches and Falls of Water, and likewise a
Fountain in the Middle [Fig. 29]; and towards the
End you are agreeably surpriz'd with a Flower-
Garden on a Slope, to which you are let thro' the
Hedge by an undiscover'd Gap; when you come
to the End of the Terras, your Prospect is so far
enlarg'd, that you see *Welch* Mountains thirty or
forty Miles distant: Here you have large arch'd
Seats, on which are painted Motto's suitable to
their Situation, and a pleasant little Garden laid
out into Gravel-Walks, Grall-Plats, &c. from
hence you advance to a Mount considerably higher
still, in the Middle of a Warren; on the Top of
which is a large Seat, call'd a *Windsor* Seat, which
is contriv'd to turn round any Way, either for the
Advantage of Prospect, or to avoid the Incon-
veniences of Wind, the Sun, &c. Here 'tis you have
a most entertaining Prospect all round, and you
see into several Counties of *England*, as well as *Wales*.

29. **The western end of the Terraces (cf. Fig. 20).**

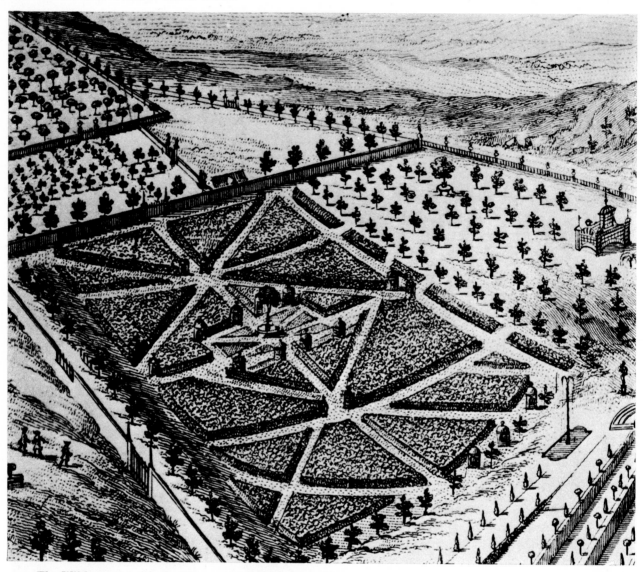

30. The Wilderness, with the Mount and Arbour beyond.

From this Seat you descend again to a flourishing Wilderness [Fig. 30], on an easy Slope, cut out into the utmost Variety of Walks, especially solitary Walks, and beautify'd with Statues: In the Middle there is a delightful square Garden, having four large Seats at the Corners, and a Seat round an aspiring Fir-Tree in the Center, from whence your Prospect terminates in a large old Church, at a very great Distance. I never in my whole Life did see so agreeable a Place for the sublimest Studies, as this is in the Summer, and here are small Desks erected in Seats for that Purpose. On one Side you ascend several Grass Steps, and come to an artificial Mount, whereon is a large spreading Tree, with a Vane at the Top, and a Seat enclosing it, commanding a most agreeable and entire Prospect of the Vale below; from hence you come down to a very magnificent Arbour, with the Convenience of Water-Works to play round it. Opposite in the Park, on a Hill of equal Elevation, is an Arbour every Way answering this [see Fig. 26], and compleats the Regularity: From hence you ascent the Mount again, and go by the Lodge and a large Nursery of Trees into the Park, where, on a Hill almost as high as any I have describ'd, is the Spring Head and the Pond, which supplies the Water-Works: It takes up near an Acre of Ground, and at the Head is eighteen or twenty Foot deep; it has an Island in the middle planted with Trees, contains Variety of the finest Water-Fowl, is well stock'd with most Sorts of Fish; and here you may sail in a Ship on a Mountain.

The National Trust and the National Art-Collections Fund

BRINSLEY FORD *Chairman of the NACF*

At our Annual Meeting in 1976 our members agreed that our Charter should be amended to give us the power to assist the National Trusts of England and of Scotland to acquire pictures and works of art for their houses.

The advantages to the National Trust of this change in our Charter are twofold. First, the best place for most works of art is the house to which they have always belonged. Many of the treasures in National Trust houses still belong to the families of the former owners of the houses, who, unfortunately, from time to time find themselves forced to sell some of them. For instance, it was most regrettable that, as the result of the Government's refusal to make a special grant, two of Largillière's beautiful portraits of the three members of the Throckmorton family who became nuns were lost to Coughton Court in Warwickshire. Other such losses are Brussels tapestries and English eighteenth-century lacquer commodes from Uppark in Sussex.

There are a great many works of art of the first importance in National Trust houses which have been retained by the family, and which might suddenly appear on the market. The National Trust has no fund available for buying works of art. The Government can accept them on its behalf in lieu of death duty, and the Trust is entitled to apply for a grant of up to fifty per cent of the purchase price from the special fund administered by the Victoria and Albert Museum. In the past the Trust would have had to raise the rest of the money by appealing to private benefactors. It must still do this if there is a large sum to be raised, but now it can also seek the aid of the NACF, and we would do our best to help, although I should stress that until we can substantially increase our capital and our membership, our contributions can never be as large as we should like. With an income of £100,000 a year, and only 10,000 members, we can be called on for assistance by any of the 700 museums in the United Kingdom.

The second way in which the amendment to our Charter allows us to help the National Trust is that we are now empowered to present to houses in its ownership works of art that have come to us either by gift or bequest. In these difficult times when, owing to financial stringencies, many of our museums have been denied their promised extensions, and their reserve sections are crammed with pictures that cannot be hung, it is more important than ever that pictures should be distributed to places where they can be seen. The National Trust owns a number of unfurnished houses such as Montacute in Somerset, Beningbrough in Yorkshire, Hatchlands near Guildford and Mompesson House in Salisbury which have room for works of art which may one day be supplied by the NACF.

In conclusion I would like to illustrate the first picture that the NACF has given to the National Trust. This is the portrait (Fig. 1) of William Michael Rossetti (brother of Dante Gabriel) by H. H. Gilchrist. It was presented to the Fund by Mrs. (Virginia) Surtees, the author of the *catalogue raisonné* of Rossetti's drawings, with the express wish that it should be given to the National Trust to be hung at Wightwick Manor near Wolverhampton. In this pre-Raphaelite house, which is lived in by Lady Mander, herself a great authority on the Movement, this portrait of one of the Brotherhood has found the perfect setting. It was painted, Mrs. Surtees informs me, in W. M. Rossetti's library at St. Edmund's Terrace, Primrose Hill, about the turn of the century, or slightly later, when he was editing the works of his brother, Dante Gabriel, whose tie-pin he is wearing and whose portrait of Jane Morris hangs on the wall behind him. The reproduction, as Mrs. Surtees points out, does not quite do justice to the picture as it gives no idea of the amber light from the fire which lights up the whole painting. And what, she asks, is the creature in the cage at the side with the beady eye – a parrot?

This is the first picture that the NACF has given the National Trust, and I hope that it will not be the last, for I am sure that our two institutions have much to be gained from being more closely linked.

1. **Portrait of William Michael Rossetti, by Herbert Harlakenden Gilchrist,** *c.* **1900. Oil on canvas 126 × 100 cm. Presented by Mrs. (Virginia) Surtees through the NACF to the National Trust, and now at Wightwick Manor, Wolverhampton.**

Notes on Contributors

Timothy Clifford, formerly a member of the Department of Ceramics at the Victoria and Albert Museum, is now Assistant Keeper of Prints and Drawings at the British Museum.

Brinsley Ford, one time Trustee of the National Gallery, is a member of the Arts panel of the National Trust, and Chairman of the National Art Collections Fund. He is an authority on English Grand Tourists in the eighteenth century, and has contributed regularly to the *Burlington Magazine*.

Joyce Godber was formerly County Archivist for Bedfordshire, and is the author of a *History of Bedfordshire* and other works; **John Manning** is an architect with special interest in the repair and maintenance of old buildings.

John Kenworthy-Browne was for a time National Trust representative in Wessex, and was the author of the catalogue for the 'Europalia' exhibition mounted by the Trust in Brussels in 1974. He has contributed regularly to *Apollo* and *Connoisseur*, chiefly on aspects of Neo-classical art, and is writing a book on the sculptor Nollekens.

Alvilde Lees-Milne was the creator of a greatly admired garden at Alderley Grange in Gloucestershire, and has always been fascinated by what inspired the makers of famous gardens of the past. For many years she lived in France, before her marriage to the writer and historian James Lees-Milne, then Architectural Adviser to the National Trust. She has herself served as a member of the Trust's Gardens Committee.

Anthony Mitchell joined the National Trust in 1965 as representative for Wessex, and is now responsible for the South West Midlands and South Wales area. He lives in one of the wings at Dyrham.

John Martin Robinson works in the Historic Buildings Division of the GLC. He became interested in the Wyatts at Oxford while writing a D. Phil. thesis on Samuel Wyatt, the architect and engineer and has recently completed a book on the whole Wyatt family, to be published shortly by the Clarendon Press.

Dr. John Smart is chairman of the Wicken Fen Local Committee of the National Trust. Until his recent retirement he was a Lecturer in Zoology and Curator of Insects in the University Museum of Zoology at Cambridge University.

Karin-M. Walton, formerly on the staff of Temple Newsam House, Leeds, is now Assistant Curator of Applied Art at Bristol City Art Gallery. Her main interest is in eighteenth century upholstery and furnishings, a subject on which she is preparing a thesis for her master's degree.

Acknowledgements

The illustrations to articles which are not credited below are the copyright of the National Trust.

Cigoli's Adoration of the Magi at Stourhead,
by Timothy Clifford
2, 3. Courtauld Institute of Art
4, 5. Caroline Coffey
6. National Gallery
7–12, 15, 16. Uffizi, Florence
13, 14. Louvre, Paris
17. Commune de Lucca
19. Cleveland Museum of Art

Lawrence Johnston, Creator of Hidcote Garden,
by Alvilde Lees-Milne
1. Daily Graphic
2. by permission of Mr. Warre
3, 4, 7. Edwin Smith
5. Peter Burton
6. A. de Rahm
9. by permission of Mr. Preston
10. by permission of Mr. J. Russell

R. J. Wyatt's 'Flora and Zephyr' at Nostell Priory,
by John Martin Robinson
1. C. C. Hutchinson
2. Alinari (The Mansell Collection)

Housekeeping in the Eighteenth and Nineteenth
Centuries, by Karin-M. Walton
1, 3. John Bethell
2. West Sussex Record Office
4, 5. d'Este Photography
6. Courtauld Institute of Art
7, 8. Jeremy Whitaker
9. *Country Life*

Wicken Fen and the Swallowtail Butterfly,
by John Smart
1–7. W. H. Palmer

Staying at Felbrigg as the Guest of Wyndham
Ketton-Cremer, by Brinsley Ford
1. A. C. Cooper
2–6 Jeremy Whitaker

Rise and Demise of a Wren Church: the Reredos from
St. Matthew Friday Street at Polesden Lacey,
by John Kenworthy-Browne
2, 3, 5–8, 15. Guildhall Library
11. National Monuments Record
13, 14. Ivor Bulmer-Thomas

Willington 'Stable': an Architectural Puzzle,
by John Manning and Joyce Godber
1. A. F. Kersting (Courtesy of Messrs. Hodder and
Stoughton)
2–4. Eric G. Meadows
5. Maps drawn by Mr. Alan Cirket
6. Department of Manuscripts, British Museum (by
permission of the Trustees)

The Park and Gardens at Dyrham,
by Anthony Mitchell
1. Edwin Smith
2. *Chipping Sodbury Gazette*
3. Gloucestershire Record Office
4. William Morris
5. Aerofilms
6. Gloucestershire Record Office
7. RIBA Drawings Collection
8. *Chipping Sodbury Gazette*
9. Gloucestershire Record Office
11. William Morris
12. Gloucestershire Record Office
20. *Country Life*
21. Angelo Hornak

The National Trust and the National Art-Collections
Fund, by Brinsley Ford
1. The Stone Gallery

Cover and layout designed by Jonathan Gill-Skelton

The National Trust Year Book 1975-76

Copies of *The National Trust Year Book* 1975–76 are still available and may be purchased from the National Trust, from Europa Publications Limited, or from bookshops. Here is a list of the essays it contains:

Caravaggesque Pictures in National Trust Houses, by Benedict Nicolson

Pritchard as Architect and Antiquary at Powis, by James Lawson and Merlin Waterson

Delft at Dyrham, by Michael Archer

The Blathwayt Brothers of Dyrham in Italy on the Grand Tour, by Brinsley Ford

The Gardens at Claremont, by Dorothy Stroud

Jan Wyck and John Wootton at Antony, by Oliver Millar

A Romano-British Site off Brownsea Island, by H. C. Bowen

Knightshayes, Devon: Burges versus Crace, by J. Mordaunt Crook

The Coastal Properties of the National Trust: Some Problems of Physiography and Conservation, by J. A. Steers

A Collection of Elizabethan and Jacobean Plays at Petworth, by Edward Miller

An Elizabethan Herbarium: Embroideries by Bess of Hardwick after the Woodcuts of Mattioli, by J. L. Nevinson

John Chute's Drawings for The Vyne, by Michael McCarthy

The National Portrait Gallery's Set of Kings and Queens at Montacute House, by Robin Gibson

A Lute Music Discovery at Lanhydrock, by Robert Spencer

A 'Norman' Wallpainting by Thomas Hopper: the Lessons of a Discovery at Penrhyn, by Merlin Waterson

Notes on the Furniture by Thomas Chippendale the Younger at Stourhead, by John Kenworthy-Browne

The Prize of Captain Hyde Parker, by David Howard

The Stourhead Batoni and other Copies after Reni, by Francis Russell

John Hungerford Pollen and his Decorative Work at Blickling Hall, by Geoffrey Fisher and Helen Smith

The National Trust Year Book 1976-77

Copies of *The National Trust Year Book* 1976–77 are still available and may be purchased from the National Trust, from Europa Publications Limited, or from bookshops. Here is a list of the essays it contains:

The Culzean Park Centre: A New Use for Robert Adam's Home Farm, by Elizabeth Beazley

Elizabethan-Revival Charlecote Revived, by John Hardy and Clive Wainwright

The Ogofau Roman Gold Mines at Dolaucothi, by P. R. Lewis

Bembridge Windmill, by Rex Wailes

The Comédie Française (Théâtre de l'Odéon): An Illustrated Discourse by de Wailly and Peyre at Waddesdon, by Allan Braham

Early Memories of Hardwick Hall and Bolsover Castle, by Sacheverell Sitwell

Murlough Nature Reserve: the Conservation of a Sand Dune System, by J. A. Whatmough

Works by Zurich Reformers in the Library at Lanhydrock, by David Keep

The Early Years of the Country Houses Scheme, by James Lees-Milne

Salvin at Dunster Castle, by Dudley Dodd

Formal Garden Designs for Cliveden: the Work of Claude Desgots and Others for the 1st Earl of Orkney, by Gervase Jackson-Stops